Love Me Tender

Love Me Tender

The stories behind the world's best-loved songs

Max Cryer

FRANCES LINCOLN LIMITED
PUBLISHERS

Frances Lincoln Limited
4 Torriano Avenue
London NW5 2RZ
www.franceslincoln.com

First published in the UK: 2008
First published in the USA: 2008

A catalogue record for this book is available from the British Library.

ISBN: 978-0-7112-2911-2

Text design and production by *BookNZ*
All photographs supplied by TRANZ International Image Library, except for those supplied by the author on the following pages: p. 22; p. 89 (copyright The Cole Porter Musical and Literary Property Trusts); p. 111. Attempts have been made to secure copyright clearances for all illustrations.

Printed and bound in Singapore

9 8 7 6 5 4 3 2 1

It makes you grin,
Gets under your skin,
As only a song can do.

'SAM'S SONG', LEW QUADLING AND JACK ELLIOTT, 1950

Author's note

The author is grateful to the following for assistance in the preparation of this book:

Jackie Blacklock, David Stevens, Lyndsay Freer, Desmond Digby, Alistair Gilkison, Paul Barrett and Ron Ince.

Contents

Introduction

The brittle character Amanda in Noel Coward's *Private Lives* makes the famous remark, 'Extraordinary how potent cheap music is.' If in her snobbish way she means 'popular', then she is right. Hearing just four notes from the opening phrase of a familiar song, or reading one line of its words, can create an immediate emotional reaction.

Behind many songs there is a story, from a ditty as simple as 'Greensleeves' right through to a rollicking, full-bore 'Hello, Dolly!'. The creation of a song can be the result of a multitude of factors – a sudden inspiration from the muse, or economic desperation: Mozart wrote *The Magic Flute* to pay off the debt collector.

Sometimes the attention of just one person can make an obscure song famous. An old melody composed by a long-dead Mexican street musician was presented to Mario Lanza with new words and became his most famous recording. Had Robert Burns not heard an old man sing a quavering version of an ancient Scottish country song, we would never have had 'Auld Lang Syne'. In 1855 Jane Ross wrote down the tune she heard played by a piper at an Irish village fair; otherwise, the rest of the world would not have heard 'Danny Boy'. Marie Antoinette heard a peasant nurse sing an obscure lullaby to her princely son and promoted it so that it is now categorised by the *Guinness Book of Records* as one of the three most familiar songs in the world. An English composer's ditty, about a blackbird singing in a tree, was sold to an American 'minstrel' show and 95 years later the song became one of Elvis Presley's biggest hits, and the title of this book.

Who knew that the American national anthem was composed by the organist of Gloucester Cathedral? Or that 'Happy Birthday' is copyright until 2030? The tune of Pepsi-Cola's television jingle was first published in Britain in 1695. Marlene Dietrich hated 'Falling in Love Again' when she first heard it, then sang it worldwide for over

40 years. Christopher Plummer's singing in *The Sound of Music* movie was dubbed by the same man who sings for Yogi Bear. Paul McCartney composed a tune to which the only words he could fit were 'scrambled eggs'; it became 'Yesterday'. And James Michener was nagged for the rest of his life with questions about the exact location of Bali Ha'i.

The 40 songs in this book are well known, popular and 'potent' – and they all have a good story behind them.

Memory

Midnight. Not a sound from the pavement.

ANDREW LLOYD WEBBER, TREVOR NUNN, T.S. ELIOT, 1981

In 1939 a slim volume of poems by T.S. Eliot was published. *Old Possum's Book of Practical Cats*, which sold for 3s 6d, whimsically told of 'Jellicle' and 'Pollicle' cats, names that came from Eliot's young godchildren trying to say 'jolly little' and 'poor little'. Fifty years after its publication, that slim volume had engendered a musical that has earned hundreds of millions of dollars.

Born in Missouri, Thomas Stearns Eliot (1888–1965) became identified as a major poet when still in his twenties. He was a friend of Ezra Pound, who called him 'Old Possum'. Eliot moved from the United States to England in 1914, and remained there for the rest of his life. As well as his intellectual and academic works, Eliot had an endearing ability to reveal a common touch; one of his fans was Groucho Marx.

British composer Andrew Lloyd Webber had become familiar with the Eliot cat poems during his childhood, when his mother would read them to him. Years later, as an adult, he spotted *Old Possum's Book of Practical Cats* at an airport bookstore, bought it and avidly refamiliarised himself with the poems. By 1977 he was contemplating the idea of setting some of them to music and discussed the matter with an eminent man of the theatre, who immediately began to picture representations of British political life among the characters – Gladstone, Queen Victoria, Disraeli. Lloyd Webber said firmly that the poems were simply about cats. Webber then told renowned theatre director Trevor Nunn that he had made some of the cat poems into songs and was wondering about them forming the nucleus of a concert song cycle, or was there a possibility that the poems could be the basis of a major new theatre musical? Nunn was deeply disappointed, and judged the idea to have only limited audience appeal.

11

There was also the matter of the poems' legal availability. They had previously been set by another composer as orchestral pieces with a spoken voice-over. Eliot himself had recorded the poems, as had actress Elsa Lanchester. And some time earlier, Eliot had turned down an approach from the Disney organisation, on the grounds that the cats in his poems were from alleys, not necessarily clean, and he didn't want to risk their being turned into cute cartoons.

The turning point occurred in 1980, by which time Lloyd Webber had set some of the poems to music, and arranged a small private performance of them. Eliot's widow, and executor, Valerie was invited to attend. She had total control over his published output so her approval was essential. After hearing the initial offerings, Valerie Eliot was warmed by Lloyd Webber's evocative treatment of the cat poems as songs. She approved of his concept and his musical style, and gave the necessary agreement for her husband's poems about cats to be turned into a musical.

Even better, she presented Webber with some unpublished fragments from Eliot's papers – incomplete verses, scribbled ideas and letters – in one of which he speculated about finishing his *Old Possum* collection with a poem about cats dancing. That poem never happened, but 40 years after the letter had been written, Eliot's idea formed the focus of a formidable group of theatre talents who became the creators of a mega-hit show in which cats sang Eliot's poems, and danced.

One fragment Valerie Eliot passed on to Lloyd Webber told of the fanciful notion that, in death, cats would travel up past the Russell Hotel and into the 'Heaviside Layer'. Another fragment was a brief but sad eight-line piece about a once-glamorous cat called Grizabella who, as the years went by, was forced to face the loss of her looks, and her own mortality. The piece had never been published; shortly before the *Old Possum* book was finalised, Eliot had removed the Grizabella character because her melancholy might affect children reading the other more lively poems.

Gradually the character of Grizabella started to form, and to become an integral part of the stage cats' street life. Webber could see that a character with pathos, and a tatty appearance, could become part of the light and shade pattern that any extended performance needs. As young and sprightly cats in spectacular costumes danced up a storm, the husky, haunting image of the aged Grizabella was on the edge of vision, a reminder to jaunty youth that a Jellicle ball didn't last for ever, and her sad and slow journey towards her end could form the only fragile suggestion of a 'plot' to hold the whole show together.

That was all very well, but Grizabella needed a defining song. At the time, Lloyd Webber had a spare melody – something he'd composed for a miniature opera about Puccini and his wife. The opera was never performed, but the melody was brought out of retirement as a possible song for Juan Peron in Webber's *Evita*. That show was certainly performed but the melody in question had been dropped. Originally, Andrew Lloyd Webber had played the tune to his father, also a composer, and asked if it sounded like Puccini. William Lloyd Webber replied that it sounded more like a million dollars.

The Puccini-type melody was revived and the new show gradually formed into a cohesive shape. In the meantime Trevor Nunn had thought carefully about his earlier opinion, and realised that Lloyd Webber's track record included two hugely successful pieces of music theatre based on unexpected subjects: the Passion of Christ, and a South American dictator's wife. Nunn told the Academy of Achievement that Lloyd Webber 'hasn't notably made mistakes in his choice of material.' This being the case, perhaps he could also be right about cats – so Nunn agreed to direct. (Later Lloyd Webber would comment on Nunn's taste for tackling theatrical problems that most people consider insoluble.)

But words were needed. Nothing appropriate to the Grizabella character presented itself in the published *Old Possum* poems. Three lyric writers were invited to survey the possibilities of modification but could not satisfy either Webber or director Trevor Nunn.

The latter made a diligent search through the rest of Eliot's published output, and his eye landed on a section of the poem 'Rhapsody on a Windy Night' from the 1917 collection, *Prufrock and Other Observations*. Here were images of midnight, a streetlamp sputtering, a cat flattening itself in a gutter to reach rancid scraps, a moon which has lost its memory … And an idea began to emerge.

Seamlessly melding together phrases from *Prufrock* into Eliot's brief separate image of the faded Grizabella, Nunn put together a lyric that perfectly fitted Webber's tune, and pleased the composer when he heard melody and words together. Slightly later, for no clear reason, Webber viewed an alternative set of lyrics written by Tim Rice, and approved those as well.

By now, the musical *Cats* was in rehearsal. Most people in theatre circles thought the concept was insane, but formidable talents were at work. Prime choreographer Gillian Lynne was training dancers to flex wrists, arch backs and leap sideways; a 'tribe' of human-sized cats was being created.

Judi Dench was engaged to play Grizabella. One of Britain's finest acting stars, her somewhat rudimentary singing voice was expressive, if not polished. She had played Sally Bowles to great acclaim in the London production of *Cabaret* and later played Desiree Armfeldt in *A Little Night Music*. But well into the rehearsal period, disaster struck. Dame Judi fell awkwardly and tore her Achilles tendon. Reinstated at rehearsals with one leg in plaster, she fell again and had to withdraw from the show. A rapid phone call was made to Elaine Page, the original Evita. Curiously, the day before she had just been listening in her car to a radio discussion about the forthcoming show *Cats*, and en route from her garage to her house had been apprehended by a stray cat, to whom she took a liking. Now came a principal role in another highly significant theatre production. She kept the stray cat, who devoted himself to her for the rest of his life.

Initially, working against time, Elaine Paige was occasionally confused between the two existing sets of words for 'Memory' – from Trevor Nunn, and from Tim Rice.

The original Grizabella, Elaine Paige.

Occasionally she sang a version that mixed the two lyrics. Eventually, however, the final decision was made, and Nunn's version prevailed.

In spite of a bomb scare on the official London opening night *Cats* was a sensation – and remained one. The London production played to full capacity for 20 years and the Broadway season had advance bookings of $10 million before it even opened, then ran for 18 years. Countless international companies presented the show to cultures as distant from Britain as Japan and Russia. The appeal of cats is universal.

The thrill of the show did not come from tunes or its simple, virtually non-existent, storyline. It came from a clever combination of age-old theatrical values, brilliant choreography and modern electronic effects, all focused on a mystery which intrigues many households in the contemporary world: what do cats think, and what do they do in their spare time? T.S. Eliot was able to provide one man's answer, and Webber's musical settings, Nunn's direction and Lynne's choreography spectacularly enhanced his words. *Cats* is a vastly entertaining piece of theatre which can be enjoyed only if you are there. Seeing the action on a screen, big or small, can never capture, or share, the magic.

The judgement about the success of *Cats* is irrevocably connected to its financial gains. In its first eight years the show was within a whisker of having generated $1 billion worth of business, and not just from ticket sales. There were souvenirs aplenty: barbecue aprons and key rings, posters, towels and tablecloths, T-shirts, nightshirts, mugs, coasters and books – all aimed at raising the kitty.

It has always been difficult to pin down the magic of *Cats*. There is no story, much of the music is rather élitist and there is precious little to hum, most of the words are unintelligible and it's set in a rubbish dump. Nevertheless, by virtue of their mysterious and elusive qualities, cats are able to grab at many a human heartstring.

Most of the music is not memorable. Except for one song. Ultimately, in the show's chill grey dawn, Old Deuteronomy is obliged to send Grizabella on her heart-wrenching ascent to the Heaviside Layer and thence to the gates of Cat Heaven. Clutching her ragged fur and a shred of faded pride, she must go before she becomes an offence to herself – and to all cats. But at least she has her 'Memory', and can 'smile at the old days' when she was beautiful and knew what happiness was.

Grizabella is the character theatre-goers remember the most. And her song is the one most often hummed, and recorded. Elaine Paige created it, Barbra Streisand followed and nearly 500 other recording artists came after them. 'Memory' became a welcome background in countless hotel foyers, shopping malls, restaurants and elevators.

The magic of cats remains paramount. It's hard to imagine there would be worldwide excitement if someone composed a musical called *Dogs*.

Love Me Tender

Love me true,
Never let me go.

GEORGE R. POULTON, VERA MATSON,
ELVIS PRESLEY, 1956

Elvis Presley might not have had one of his hit records if the Poulton family hadn't left England in 1835 to seek a new life in America. They settled in Lansburgh, New York where young George learned violin and piano, and hoped to move into conducting. At the age of 12 he also tried fledgling composing, and over the following two decades had more then 20 songs published.

It was the age of minstrel shows, which often featured jaunty upbeat songs. With this in mind, Poulton composed a tune, with words by lyricist William Whiteman Fosdick, which would be a contrast – a simple sentimental ballad with the highly traditional theme of a beautiful young woman with shining hair. They called the song 'Aura Lee' and when the music was published and copyrighted in Cincinnati in 1861 it carried a dedication to the Holley and Campbell Minstrels.

As the blackbird in the spring,
'Neath the willow tree
Sat and pip'd I heard him sing
Sing-ing Aura Lee.
Aura Lee! Aura Lee!
Maid of golden hair;
Sunshine came along with thee,
And swallows in the air.

16

Although 'Aura Lee' was successful as a minstrel song, it also gained unexpected popularity with the trainee soldiers at West Point, where it quickly became a graduating class song and gained new words (by L.W. Becklaw), soon becoming known as 'Army Blue'. The song was also known later as 'The Violet' and 'The Girl with the Golden Hair'.

The timing was crucially relevant to the song's future; soon after 'Aura Lee' was released, the American Civil War began.

Music is often part of war. Certain music gains a special currency among the combatants – and so it was with this conflict. Drums, fifes, fiddles, banjos and brass were played by camp fires, at ceremonies, while marching – and even during battle. Solo singers and troops *en masse* sang songs declaring patriotic loyalty (according to which side was singing), songs of yearning for a faraway love, upbeat lively numbers for raising the spirits, more sombre reflections on the bleakness of war and the sad strains of burial. 'Aura Lee' became a favourite for troops on both sides of the conflict. The image of the lovely girl was even added to another war song, 'The Yellow Rose of Texas':

Talk about your Clementine
Or sing of Aura Lee.

After the war, 'Aura Lee' was taken up by barber-shop quartets and later recorded by many artists, but its military connection still hovered. In the 1936 movie *Come and Get It*, Frances Farmer sang it as two different characters in two different voices (she played a mother and daughter). It reappeared in *The Last Musketeer* (1952) and *The Long Grey Line* used it as a West Point song, under the titles, in 1955. Only one year later, George Poulton's melody was to be launched to a much wider international audience.

An entertainment phenomenon called Elvis Presley had caused musical hysteria with his recording of 'Blue Suede Shoes', a hysteria which continued and constantly gained momentum, through 'Heartbreak Hotel', then 'Hound Dog'. With the royalties from these successes, Elvis bought a roomy new house in Audubon Drive, Memphis (not Graceland – that came later) and having reached impressive heights in recording and television studios, started to cast his eye on a possible movie career.

With the doubtful guidance of 'Colonel' Tom Parker, a Dutch immigrant made an honorary colonel for helping a state election campaign, in 1956 Elvis was contracted into his first-ever role, in a movie to be called *Love Me Tender*. And it was decided that, in the movie, he would sing his first-ever non-rock ballad.

So a song was needed. Music director on the movie was Ken Darby, who eventually found the 95-year-old melody 'Aura Lee'. Poulton's simple tune needed no restructuring,

Elvis was already becoming a legend when he made his first movie.

but new words seemed to be called for. It is believed that Darby himself was responsible for the revised lyrics, but he gave the credits to his wife Vera Matson – and Presley. So was born the song 'Love Me Tender'.

Elvis recorded it in August 1956 on a large sound stage without his usual band and back-up singers. The second take was declared satisfactory, and 'Love Me Tender' was unleashed on a Presley-enthusiastic world. Very quickly it became the top *Billboard* pop single, remaining No. 1 for five weeks and staying in the chart list for 23 weeks. Its popularity wasn't restricted to the pop single market: 'Love Me Tender' also appeared as a success on the R&B and country music charts.

Presley and his manager had no compunction about rearranging existing songs to suit themselves; several of his other hits arose from similar borrowings. 'Wooden Heart' was a combination of new English words added to the German tune 'Muss Ich denn', the French 'Plaisir d' Amour' became 'Can't Help Falling in Love' and 'It's Now or Never' was a rewrite of Italy's 'O Sole Mio'.

After Presley, other artists stepped up to the recording mike with 'Love Me Tender':

Connie Francis, The Platters, Tony Bennett, Marty Robbins, Kenny Rogers, Engelbert Humperdinck, Paul Anka, Ray Conniff, The Lettermen, Linda Ronstadt, even Frank Sinatra. It was difficult, however, to escape the shadow cast by Presley's intimate and huskily crooned performance.

Although launched in a much heralded movie, the song completely outclassed the film, which is generally considered an artistic non-event. George Poulton died in 1867, before he turned 40. He never knew that within less than a century, his simple tune 'Aura Lee' would become familiar to a large proportion of the developed world.

You ain't nothin' but a hound dog . . .

Willie Mae 'Big Mama' Thornton was a blues singer of large physique, a dominating presence and a thunderstorm voice. Mike Stoller and Jerry Lieber were two young writers who wanted to compose a song that would sit well with the singer's formidable charisma: something involving a lot of shouting and commanding seemed appropriate. In 1952 they came up with a short piece in which a woman gave a very definite dismissal to a lover. They called it 'Hound Dog', a term that was seen as a possible euphemism for gigolo, then considered an unacceptable word for broadcast.

'Hound Dog' began life being written on the back of a paper bag, and was transformed by Thornton into a vocal display of slow but energetic passion, including barking, howling and bellowed instruction to the band to wag their tails. Her record was top of the American R&B charts for seven weeks in 1953.

Three years later Elvis Presley was in Las Vegas and heard Freddie Bell perform the number. Within a week Presley had added it to his own act, and recorded it soon after. 'Hound Dog' became an instant phenomenon, even though by now the song had undergone some modifications from Thornton's original. Presley's first performance of the song on television was seen by 40 million people and caused an uproar of criticism, including terms like 'caterwaul' and 'no talent'. His next television performance was seen by an even bigger audience and he sang the song to a basset hound wearing a top hat.

When the liner *Andrea Doria* sank near Nantucket, Massachusetts in July 1956 one survivor was writer Mike Stoller, who was collected at the New York pier by his co-writer, Jerry Lieber, with the news that their song 'Hound Dog' had become a major hit – not the Big Mama Thornton record, but a new cover version by a kid called Elvis Presley. Stoller said, 'Elvis who?'

Edelweiss

Every morning you greet me.

RICHARD RODGERS AND OSCAR HAMMERSTEIN II, 1959

In 1925, widowed naval commander Baron Georg Ritter von Trapp asked a Salzburg convent near his home if anyone was available to teach a sickly child – one of seven children. His wife had died of scarlet fever three years before. Young Maria Kutschera was a candidate for the novitiate but was also a qualified teacher, so the convent arranged that she would be a resident governess to the von Trapps for nine months.

The new governess found that she was the twenty-sixth in a long line of governesses, teachers and nurses in the von Trapp household. The father was striving to keep the home as happy and lively as possible, singing with his children and telling fireside stories. Gradually the reserve melted between the older aristocratic military captain and the 21-year-old governess and after two years with the family, she married the baron. Three more children were born, bringing the total to 10.

In 1935 financial disaster befell the family. To oblige a family friend, Baron von Trapp had transferred his capital from an English bank to an Austrian one, but under increasing economic pressure (partly from Germany) the bank collapsed, taking the von Trapp money with it. Baron and Baroness were obliged to dismiss servants and take in lodgers. By then, encouraged by Baroness Maria, the family's hobby of singing together had evolved into a pleasing vocal sound, which seemed a possible way of earning income. Unwilling though he was for his family to appear in public as singers, Georg von Trapp agreed. One year after their financial disaster, the von Trapp family competed in the Salzburg Musical Festival, won first place, and were then able to take singing engagements further afield.

During the following decade the von Trapps were encouraged by opera star

Elisabeth Schumann to take their singing further than just their home and the family became transformed into a successful singing group. But the idyll came to an end when the Nazi shadow began to loom close to Austria. The von Trapps, loyal to their homeland, were determined not to be part of the German insistence on annexing Austria. In 1938, feeling sad and apprehensive, the family made a discreet departure from Salzburg on a seemingly innocent train trip. Eventually they reached the United States, where the Trapp Family Choir (later the Trapp Family Singers) became established as international concert performers.

In 1956 a German movie told the family's story. Two years later the Paramount movie organisation in Hollywood considered remaking the movie, with Audrey Hepburn as Maria von Trapp, but time went by and their legal option to reconstruct the German movie lapsed. Then Broadway star Mary Martin happened to see the script for the intended Paramount movie, and there arose the suggestion of a theatre musical version.

The genesis was slow. It took a year to locate all the genuine von Trapp children, now adults, and the Baroness Maria herself was eventually found in New Guinea establishing a Christian mission. Besides that project, the now widowed baroness was running a 'family hotel' in Vermont, which Mary Martin visited; from Baroness Maria she learned to play guitar and to genuflect.

Rodgers and Hammerstein took only six months to write the score and lyrics for the intended musical. To create the role of Baron von Trapp they found Theodore Bikel, an accomplished folk singer and later a renowned Tevye in *Fiddler on the Roof*. Bikel was also Austrian-born, so felt some affinity with Baron von Trapp. He was performing in Holland when asked to audition for the new musical, and flew to New York especially to sing to Rodgers and Hammerstein. Fortunately, so he later believed, he brought his guitar with him, and accompanied himself for a couple of items during his audition session. Theatre legend has it that after he'd finished and left the stage, Mary Martin whispered to Rodgers, 'We don't have to look any further, do we?'

As is usual, once the new musical, *The Sound of Music*, was ready, it had try-out performances away from New York. Only two weeks before the scheduled Broadway opening date, a feeling had grown that there should be a song for the leading man.

The storyline of *The Sound of Music* had taken major liberties with the truth. The real Baron von Trapp was not an unfeeling, regimenting father, but lively and affectionate with the children, and they all left Austria on a train, not by climbing a mountain. But the attraction between the Baron and the governess was certainly true, as was the baron's love of the alpine flower, edelweiss – and the fact that he could sing.

Rodgers and Hammerstein set out to create a song about the edelweiss, whose name translates as 'noble and white'. The song's gentle 3/4 time signature seemed to refer to the Austrian folk dance, the *laendler*, ancestor of the waltz rhythm. Ideally it would be sung accompanied by guitar. The result was a gentle ballad with Richard Rodgers' haunting melody, and words from the terminally ill Oscar Hammerstein – the last lyrics he ever wrote. Theodore Bikel debuted the song 'Edelweiss' (with guitar) on Broadway on 16 November 1959. To some, it seemed poignant that the final word of the song was 'forever'.

Baron Georg and Baroness Maria von Trapp.

Theodore Bikel, Mary Martin and the Rodgers and Hammerstein score brought the Trapps to life in such a way that audiences flocked to the show, not only in New York, but all over the world. Inevitably plans for a musical movie began to evolve. Rumours went round that Doris Day was being considered to play Maria von Trapp, or possibly Shirley Jones or Leslie Caron, but the producers settled on British soprano Julie Andrews, to whom the real Baroness Maria gave a lesson in yodelling.

Gossip placed Sean Connery as heading the list of possibles to play Baron von Trapp, along with Yul Brynner, Richard Burton and Bing Crosby. Apart from Crosby, then in his mid-sixties, none was a singer. Theodore Bikel was a very experienced singer, but not a front-line movie star. Neither was the Canadian actor Christopher Plummer, but he had an elegant appearance, aristocratic bearing, a commanding presence and a fine reputation as a Shakespearean leading man. The role went to him.

His singing, however, was something of a worry. Plummer started out planning to use his own voice in the movie, and he recorded the baron's singing tracks. But by the time he listened to the playbacks, he had heard the crystalline sounds of Julie Andrews, and sensibly decided that his singing voice couldn't match hers. The movie retained some of his *sprechgesang* introductions, but overdubbed his actual singing with the pleasing baritone of actor/singer Bill Lee, who had previously provided the singing voice for Lieutenant Cable in *South Pacific*, besides numerous cartoon soundtracks: *Tom and Jerry, 101 Dalmatians, The Lady and the Tramp*, and the singing voice of *Yogi Bear*. (A rare track of 'Edelweiss', sung by Plummer himself, from his own recording sessions for the movie before his singing was dropped, surfaced years later on a DVD called *Hollywood Screen Tests*.)

Edelweiss, the 'noble white' flower of the mountains.

'Edelweiss' took on a life of its own. It was so perfect within the context of the show that many people mistakenly thought it was a genuine Austrian folk tune – even perhaps the Austrian national anthem, though its waltz rhythm would make it a most unlikely choice.

In February 1984, President Rudolf Kirchschlager of Austria visited the White House and Baroness von Trapp was among the guests. While speaking of the United States' relationship with Austria, President Reagan said:

Your visit is a celebration of something real, tangible, and enduring: the friendship between the people of Austria and the people of the United States. At one point in *The Sound of Music*, the character who plays Baron von Trapp sings a song about the edelweiss, an Austrian flower. And before the song ends, the lyrics become a prayer for Austria itself. It is a prayer Americans join in – 'Blossom of snow, may you bloom and grow – and bless your homeland forever'.

So, not a national anthem, but in a comforting gesture of approval 'Edelweiss' began to feature in the concerts and recordings of the Vienna Boys' Choir.

For a short period during the 1970s, 'Edelweiss' assumed a new guise in the United States when the United Methodist Women's Conference issued a set of words for a Christian benediction, to be sung to the tune. So attractive was the result that other denominations took up the idea, and the new benediction sprouted across the States as freely as edelweiss on a mountain side. When they got to hear about it, lawyers for the estates of Rodgers and Hammerstein were not amused, and issued information that any church continuing to use the copyright material would be sued for plagiarism. The Methodist women, and those who followed them, may have been acting in innocence. Sometimes a song seeps into our minds and memories as if it had somehow 'evolved', without seeming to have been 'written' at all. 'Edelweiss' is such a song.

For He's A Jolly Good Fellow

For he's a jolly good fellow
And so say all of us.

Anon.

One of Marie Antoinette's lesser known claims to fame is that she was directly responsible for the song 'For He's a Jolly Good Fellow' eventually becoming internationally famous.

The origins of the ditty have been traced by scholars back to 11th-century France, where the ancient *Chanson de Gestes* told about a character known as Malbrouck, an heroic young man who could change form into any creature he wished. A jaunty tune with words telling of his exploits surfaced in several parts of Europe. Some scholars claim its ancestry goes as far back as *The Song of Solomon* and was known to Arabs in Palestine as well as the citizens of France and Spain. In time, tensions between England and France focused French attention on England's mighty general the Duke of Marlborough and eventually the name of the medieval French character Malbrouck came to represent Marlborough. Around France in the early 1700s, the ancient ditty about the adventures of Malbrouck took on a new life as 'Marlbrouck s'en va-t-en guerre': Marlborough's going off to war.

In 1781, when a peasant woman named Genevieve was engaged at the court of Louis XVI as cradle nurse to a royal baby, she sang her version of the old French song as a lullaby. Queen Marie Antoinette, who was Austrian and had never heard the song before, was taken with the catchy tune. She learned the song, drew the king's attention to it and encouraged its being sung around the royal court, which made it 'fashionable'. Soon almost everyone in France knew it and the song was being inscribed on fans and screens.

The song had already been printed, in a collection of French street songs, *Chansons, Vaudevilles et Ariettes*, published sometime before 1778, but the interest shown by Marie Antoinette and the court brought it much wider attention and the old song now stretched to some 18 verses. Napoleon Bonaparte was heard to hum the tune, and in his play *The Marriage of Figaro* Pierre de Beaumarchais had the character of Cherubino sing it.

'Marlbrouck s'en va-t-en guerre' became so popular throughout France that it formed the basis for comic songs in theatre revues. Its brief melody became so

Marie Antoinette, Queen of France, made the tune popular.

closely associated with the French that in 1813 Beethoven included the tune in his Opus 91, 'Wellington's Victory' (the so-called Battle Symphony), referring to the defeat of the French by the allied forces under the Duke of Wellington, at Vitoria in Spain. Frequent use of the ditty throughout the Continent made it inevitable that the British would eventually pick it up.

In Britain, and later in America, the melody seeped into fairly wide use without necessarily having any words. In England the tune was used as a harpsichord exercise, or an instrumental solo for junior violin and flute players. Across the Atlantic, its main early use was as a fife and drum piece. For a brief while British singers attached some words about a maid from Primrose Hill to the tune, and in America the tune was heard with the words 'Molly Brooks come out of the water, Until you learn to swim'. But by the 19th century the words 'For he's a jolly good fellow' had appeared from an unknown source – and those words stayed.

Although Americans cheerfully accept the very English-sounding phrase 'jolly good fellow', a curious dichotomy grew over the remaining words. The British invariably sing 'and so say all of us', but Americans equally invariably sing 'which nobody can deny'.

This phrase, 'which nobody can deny', had originated in Britain and was in use at least since the reign of Elizabeth I in contexts other than 'Jolly Good Fellow'. It was the title of a folk song sung to an old tune we now know as 'Greensleeves'. References to the expression crop up throughout 16th-, 17th- and 18th-century England. Diarist Samuel Pepys used the term in 1660 and poet William Cowper in 1788, by which time Benjamin Franklin was using it as well.

But this is not the only variation known in the song. In 1842 an American publisher put out a song arranged by musician William Clifton, drawn from the same ancient French tune:

> We're all met here together,
> We're all met here together,
> We're all met here together,
> To eat and drink good cheer;
>
> For we won't go home till morning,
> We won't go home till morning,
> We won't go home till morning,
> Till daylight does appear.

It is sung to the tune of 'Jolly Good Fellow' and in the United States at least is almost as familiar as its progenitor. A later entry was the whimsical 'The Bear Went Over the Mountain (to see what he could see)', which came into being during the 1930s and has also become very familiar in the United States.

One possible development didn't take place. A women's organisation once considered that the words 'jolly good fellow' were a bit suspect, possibly indicating alcohol and raunchy behaviour. It was therefore proposed that a more appropriate wording would be 'For They are Excellent Ladies'. Somehow it never caught on.

The Star-spangled Banner

Oh, say, can you see by, the dawn's early light,
What so proudly we hailed at the twilight's last gleaming?

FRANCIS SCOTT KEY, JOHN STAFFORD SMITH, 1814

English musician John Stafford Smith (1750–1836), the son of the organist at Gloucester Cathedral in Britain, became a choir member of the Chapel Royal and later its organist. From this somewhat rarefied musical background, Smith wrote the tune that was to become the American national anthem.

Besides performing, Smith was an active composer of anthems, glees and songs, one of which, 'To Anacreon in Heaven', was dedicated to the sixth-century Greek lyric poet Anacreon, whose poems, called anacreontics, celebrated wine and jollity. Smith's song, either composed entirely by him, or suggested by existing melodies, was published in London in 1778. Somewhat bawdy, the 'Anacreontic Song' became the theme song for societies dedicated to musicmaking, and was sung at all meetings of the music-orientated Anacreontic societies, both in Britain and later in America. The melody remained the same in America, but there the song acquired several versions of its lyrics, differing greatly from the original. The most famous version came about after war began between Britain and America in 1812.

When the British invaded Washington in 1814, a young American lawyer and poet called Francis Scott Key had left Baltimore intending to secure the release of a friend who was detained by the British fleet. But he was himself detained on a British ship during the British bombardment of the star-shaped Fort McHenry, Baltimore. Helpless, he was obliged to watch the attack take place. As night fell, Key could hear the bombshells but when day broke on 14 September, he could see the American flag still flying over the fort.

Jutting out into Baltimore Harbour, Fort McHenry had been built in the shape of a five-point star in 1805 to defend Baltimore against enemy attack. Each point of the star was fortified with the capability of cannon and musket fire.

Inspired by the Americans' brave defence of the fort, Key, still a prisoner on the British ship, started to write a poem on the back of a letter he found in his pocket. The poem began, 'Oh, say, can you see, By the dawn's early light ...'. When released, he moved into a hotel and finished his poem, called 'Defence of Fort McHenry'. Key was familiar with the Anacreon song and had already written another poem with similar rhythm. Either consciously or unconsciously, his new poem was also written in a metre which could easily be sung to that tune. He gave the poem to his brother-in-law, Joseph Nicholson, a judge, who quickly ascertained that the poem and the existing British melody would fit together. He immediately had copies of the poem printed as pamphlets, adding the heading 'Tune: Anacreon in Heaven' to the words.

Within days, 17 newspapers reprinted the poem, with the note about the tune, but by the time the sheet music containing Key's words and the Smith tune was published, the title had morphed into 'The Star-spangled Banner'. A month after it

Notable 'Star-spangled Banner' performances in modern times

- Jimi Hendrix's guitar solo at the first Woodstock festival in 1969. With massive and unsettling echo effects, interpreted by some to be resonant reminders of the contentious Vietnam War of the time, the anthem's performance became even more riveting, in the later-released movie, when seen in close-up.

- The BBC serial television production of *The Hitchhiker's Guide to the Galaxy* used a strange and rather distorted version of John Stafford Smith's tune as the Betelgeusean death song.

- The 2006 mock documentary movie *Borat: Cultural Learnings of America for Make Benefit Glorious Nation of Kazakhstan* featured the anthem in a bizarre sequence, filmed in front of a genuine rodeo audience in the United States. British actor Sasha Baron Cohen, presenting himself as a journalist from Kazakhstan being filmed for a documentary 'Visiting America', was invited to sing his nation's national anthem to the rodeo crowd. To everyone's horror he sang a mangled version of 'The Star-spangled Banner', encouraged Americans to continue fighting in Iraq and spurred the president on to 'drink blood'. Cohen escaped the outraged crowd safely and the completed sequence appeared in his Oscar-nominated film.

was first seen, 'The Star-spangled Banner' was sung in public by talented local actor Ferdinand Durang, and a legend was born. The legend started to gain formality when the American Navy made 'The Star-spangled Banner' its official flag-raising tune, and gradually other military events began to use the song. It started to become part of the 4th of July celebration, and by 1897 the song was being played at the opening of sporting events.

The star-shaped Fort McHenry in Baltimore inspired the words of the American national anthem.

America was in no hurry to accept the concept of a national anthem. Britain had been using 'God Save the King' as an anthem since the coronation of William IV in 1831, but the American government did not make a similar decision until exactly 100 years later. In 1931 Herbert Hoover joined the United States to the other nations of the world who had an official anthem, and 'The Star-spangled Banner' was elevated to official level. Some saw it as a wry irony that the nation from which America was in the process of casting itself adrift had engendered the music which eventually became the new nation's defining song. Neither nation has shown the least resentment over this.

What has been slightly more of a problem is that John Stafford Smith's tune has a range of one and a half octaves, rather more than most members of the public are able to manage. Several thousand Welsh lustily singing 'Men of Harlech' or an impassioned French crowd delivering the 'Marseillaise' make an impact, but that effect is hard to match when a tune requires more vocal stretch than the American man in the street can provide. Although the American anthem is popular and rousing, many important occasions take no risks, and bring in a professional singer to showcase the anthem as a stirring, and well-sung, solo.

By permission of the government, an American flag flies permanently over Francis Scott Key's grave in Maryland. The old 50-foot-long American flag, which Francis Scott Key saw flying over Fort McHenry by the dawn's early light on 14 September 1814, can now be seen by everyone, in the Washington History Museum. The original manuscript of the poem, 'Defence of Fort McHenry', was sold for $24,000 in New York in 1933, and two copies of the original printed word-pamphlet are held by the Maryland Historic Society.

Danny Boy

The pipes, the pipes are calling …

FRED WEATHERLY, TUNE ANON., 1913

In the Irish county of Londonderry, Jane Ross, an unmarried woman of 41, loved old-time melodies and folk music, and had collected over 100 of them. One was a melody she was reputed to have heard played by a street musician passing through the town of Limavady, where she lived.

In due time, Jane Ross passed the songs she had accumulated to a collector more dynamic than herself, who was planning to publish an anthology of the old tunes. The result, in 1855, was a book entitled *Ancient Music of Ireland*, collected by George Petrie. Among the melodies was the first printing of a tune with no name, which was included in a group simply identified as 'anonymous airs'. In an explanatory note, Petrie acknowledged the rich tradition of County Londonderry as genuinely Irish and unsullied by its infusion of settlers from England and Scotland, and thanked Jane Ross for the use of her collected melodies, particularly the 'anonymous air' which, she had told him, was 'very old'.

The tune became popular, and Jane Ross's story of its collection unchallenged. It took some 40 years before the name 'Londonderry Air' was applied to it, or sometimes 'Air from County Derry'. But a growing interest in the heritage of Irish melodies caused some doubts to hover over the provenance Ross had offered for the tune.

Apart from the old joke about its title, 'London Derriere', other parodies abound:

Oh, Paddy boy, the pints, the pints are calling,
From pub to pub, within five minutes' ride.

Oh Danny Boy, when Irish eyes were smiling
It was before they ever heard of you.

It is not clear from whom Jane Ross first heard the tune. Legend says it was either a piper, a harpist or a fiddler. But whichever was correct, musicologists were starting to wonder whether the melody was within the usual structure of Irish music. Apparently it was not, and the song's shape and rhythm did not indicate the likelihood of attached lyrics, in the way of traditional Irish folk singing. Perhaps, said sceptics, Jane Ross composed it herself, and passed it off as traditional. Of course, if that were the case, she would have missed out on massive royalties in later years – an eccentricity that would have surpassed even the Irish gift for the unexpected.

Some years after Petrie's collection, a similar tune called 'Drimoleague Fair' appeared in a Chicago publication. But the 'composer', Francis O'Neill, was suspected of having supplied a new name to the existing tune he'd seen in Petrie's book. Music scholar Anne Geddes Gilchrist wondered if perhaps the tune, as heard by Jane Ross, had been written down wrongly in 4/4 time instead of 3/4 time. This would have brought it more into line with other Irish folk tunes.

And indeed in 1979 a detailed examination of ancient melodies taken down by scholar Edward Bunting revealed that if 'Londonderry Air' had been written down incorrectly, it was fairly clearly related to the tune 'Aislean an Oigfear' ('The Young Man's Dream'), which had been 'collected' in 1792 from harpist Denis O'Hampsey. He was over 90 at the time, and had played it for years. So Jane Ross was right all along: the tune was Irish, and it was old.

There were numerous attempts to bring words to the lovely melody and make it an equally lovely song. Years before Miss Ross heard (or misheard) it, Irish poet Thomas Moore had made a completely forgotten attempt to write lyrics for the ancient tune. After Petrie published the melody, various sets of lyrics were attached to it, resulting in songs called 'Erin's Apple Blossom', 'Emer's Farewell', 'The Irish Love Song'

There is an ambiguity in the lyrics of 'Danny Boy'. It is generally assumed that the 'pipes are calling' refers to Danny being summoned, either to recruitment or actual duty, by the military sounds of pipe and drum. Pipes were either fifes or possibly bagpipes. But difficulties have arisen when translating the words into other languages. The French version sticks with 'pipe', which suggest the kind in which tobacco is smoked. The most commonly seen Spanish and Italian translations use the words that mean the type of pipes found in bathroom plumbing, and German uses a word that sits somewhere between 'valve' and the 'barrel of a gun'.

and 'In Derry Vale'. Each created a minor flurry of interest, then faded completely from sight. Nearly 100 sets of lyrics to 'The Londonderry Air' saw the light of day, but only one survived.

During the Great Famine in Ireland from 1845 to 1849, the tide of emigrants pouring into America included many Irish musicians, who of course took their music and played it in their new country. Edward Weatherly was a London doctor whose brother Fred was a prominent lawyer in Somerset. In 1899 Edward left England to live in San Francisco and later Colorado. There, amid the gold rush, his wife Margaret Weatherly heard a gold prospector playing a beautiful tune. Margaret knew that her brother-in-law Fred had a great interest in writing song lyrics, but not tunes. She politely persuaded the gold prospector to let her arrange a copy of his tune and immediately sent it to her brother-in-law in England.

Pipe-maker Eugene Lamb in County Galway with a modern Irish Uilleann pipe, virtually unchanged since they called Danny to war from glen to glen.

Fred Weatherly was a remarkable man. An eminent lawyer, he knew men who had survived the Battle of Trafalgar, he was personally acquainted with Charles Dickens and William Gladstone and he declined an offer from the King of Siam to go to Bangkok as tutor to the Crown Prince (thus depriving the world of a musical called *The King and Fred*). He had a lifelong interest in writing song lyrics: he was responsible for some 1500 published works. One of his most famous, 'Up from Somerset', was the result of a visit to London to see the Great Exhibition of 1851 and helped to establish the image of the West Country and its distinctive accent. Fred Weatherley also wrote the words for 'The Holy City' and the poignant First World War song, 'Roses of Picardy'. He collaborated with the famous Italian composer Paolo Tosti in a series of songs, and the two men sang to Queen

Victoria at a party for her jubilee in 1897. He also translated operas into English, and wrote and published children's stories. Beatrix Potter's first appearance in print was as the artist who drew the sketches in a book of poems by Fred Weatherly called *The Happy Pair*. Fred Weatherly was very busy.

By one of those coincidences that bring a glow to history, sitting in Fred Weatherly's desk drawer was a song lyric he had written several years before but had never got round to showing to a composer. It was called 'Danny Boy'. When out of the blue he received a tune-without-words from his brother's wife in America, he tentatively tried his lyrics with it. Good fortune followed good luck: with only small modifications, the words and music seemed made for each other. The combination was published in 1913.

'Danny Boy' rapidly caught the attention of Irish people in all parts of the world. Miraculously, it evoked no hint of the geographical, religious or political abrasiveness that sometimes affects Irish sensibilities. 'Danny Boy' belonged to all the Irish. People either didn't know, or preferred not to mention, that lyricist Fred Weatherly had never set foot in Ireland. In 1915 the American-based opera star Ernestine Schumann-Heink recorded 'Danny Boy' and in that era of sparse recording facilities, her stellar performance influenced nearly 200 other artists to make recordings of the song, long before recording became electrical.

When the Roman Catholic Bishop of Providence, New Jersey, banned 'Danny Boy' from funeral masses, a police officer wrote that he wanted the song to be sung at his funeral mass, and if it wasn't, he planned to get up and walk out.

Percy Grainger, Frank Bridge and Charles Villiers Stanford made instrumental arrangements of the tune, which became the basis for hymns in cathedrals and a favourite with military bands. It has also been sung on pub crawls, after-match sports gatherings, birthdays, farewells, movie soundtracks, banquets, reunions, mayoral receptions, wakes, even weddings, and in modern times, has become a karaoke standby. Pop stars and opera stars present their versions, as do church choirs, schoolchildren, nuns, road workers, choral societies, football teams, hikers and soldiers. Bing Crosby crooned it, Judy Garland sang it *a capella*, Johnny Cash, Harry Connick Jr., Dennis Day, Sinead O'Connor, Mario Lanza, Harry Belafonte, Tony Bennett, Cher, Willie Nelson, Kiri Te Kanawa and Elvis Presley all sang it in their various ways.

The song's words suggest it is to be sung by a woman – 'Danny boy, I love you so'

– but a few years after its first printing, alternative words were included if a man wanted to sing it:

EILY DEAR
words Fred E. Weatherly, written to an old Irish air

Oh, Eily dear, the pipes, the pipes are calling
From glen to glen, and down the mountain side
The summer's gone, and all the roses falling
It's I, it's I must go, and you must bide.

But I'll come back when summer's in the meadow
Or when the valley's hushed and white with snow
And you'll be here in sunshine or in shadow.
Oh Eily dear, oh Eily dear, I love you so.

But the original can easily be assumed to be brother singing to brother, or father to son, so the other version faded from view and men freely sing the original without embarrassment.

DANNY BOY

Oh Danny boy, the pipes, the pipes are calling
From glen to glen, and down the mountain side
The summer's gone, and all the flowers are dying
'tis you, 'tis you must go and I must bide.

But come you back when summer's in the meadow
Or when the valley's hushed and white with snow
'tis I'll be there in sunshine or in shadow
Oh Danny boy, oh Danny boy, I love you so.

And if you come, when all the flowers are dying
And I am dead, as dead I well may be
You'll come and find the place where I am lying
And kneel and say an 'Ave' there for me.

And I shall hear, tho' soft you tread above me
And all my dreams will warm and sweeter be
If you'll not fail to tell me that you love me
I'll simply sleep in peace until you come to me.

Oxford Professor of Music Sir Hubert Parry, speaking of Irish folk music, referred to 'Danny Boy' as a simple emotional type, and decreed that it was 'one of the most perfect in existence'.

The song is frequently performed at funerals. Actor Carol O'Connor, President John Kennedy, Elvis Presley and Diana, Princess of Wales were all laid to rest accompanied by the famous melody. Diana's funeral in Westminster Abbey featured the abbey choristers with words by Howard Arnold Walter, to 'An Air from County Derry':

I would be true, for there are those that trust me.
I would be pure, for there are those that care.
I would be strong, for there is much to suffer.
I would be brave, for there is much to dare.
I would be friend of all, the foe, the friendless.
I would be giving, and forget the gift,
I would be humble, for I know my weakness,
I would look up, and laugh, and love, and live.

I would be faithful through each passing moment;
I would be constantly in touch with God;
I would be strong to follow where He leads me;
I would have faith to keep the path Christ trod.
Who is so low that I am not his brother?
Who is so high that I've no path to him?
Who is so poor I may not feel his hunger?
Who is so rich I may not pity him?

Auld Lang Syne

Should auld acquaintance be forgot.

ROBBIE BURNS, TUNE ANON., 1796

At midnight on any New Year's Eve, millions of English-speaking people all over the world suddenly break into a phrase of ancient Scottish dialect. The occasion would not be complete without it.

The phrase in question is from Lallans, a Scots–English version of the word Lowlands, referring to that region's way of speaking English, but coloured by a distinctive Scottish vernacular. 'Auld lang syne' is the Lallans way of saying 'old long since' – times long past, or perhaps 'the good old days'.

The expression first appeared in print in 1568. Two hundred years later, the expression may have been fading from use, as many old dialect expressions do. But in 1788 Scotland's most famous poet, Robert Burns, heard an old man use the term in a quavering song, which Burns, an expert on Scottish folk poetry and songs, realised, with wonder, had never been 'taken down' before. As Dr John Cairney explains in his *Burns Companion*, the poet acknowledged from the start that he was not the originator of the phrase 'auld lang syne'; in fact Burns described it as a 'glorious fragment' invented some time in the past by a heaven-inspired poet.

Pepsi-Cola's advertising jingle 'Pepsi Cola Hits the Spot' used a tune whose origins have been traced back to Britain in 1695, when it appeared in a music volume called *The Dancing Master*, as 'Red House'. Referred to by musicologists as a 'border rant' of Scottish origin, the melody has also been used for the song 'Bonnie Annie' and most famously as the tune for the hunting song 'D'Ye Ken John Peel?'.

Several earlier poets, dating back to Sir Robert Aytoun in the early 1600s, had used the phrase in verse. But it was Robert Burns' inclusion of the phrase in a simple but resonant poem in 1788 which set 'Auld Lang Syne' on the path to gaining recognition throughout the world. All the previous versions faded into oblivion.

Burns enlarged the phrase he heard into a poem of five verses and a repeated chorus and structured the verbal sentiments into the rhythm of an old tune. It was not necessarily exactly the same tune the old man had sung but Burns had as fine an ear for music as he had for dialect and seems to have landed on an old air that fitted the words even more satisfactorily. Exactly *which* old air Burns used is not entirely clear. Marrying poetry to unattributed 'folk tunes' is a practice so old that there is little profit in worrying if the exact melody cannot be identified. Nevertheless, scholars assiduously attempt to do so.

Maurice Lindsay's *Burns Encyclopaedia* traces an early recognition of the tune in a violin solo from the 1690 musical work, 'Apollo's Banquet', which may well have drawn on excerpts from existing folk melodies, without acknowledging the sources. Nearly a century later, a lively folk tune known as either 'The Miller's Wedding' or 'The Miller's Daughter', seems a likely source for the melody Burns brought to mind for his 'Auld Lang Syne' verses, and a fragment of that same tune appears briefly in William Shield's ballad opera *Rosina*, which played at Covent Garden about 1782. In the way of such operas, Shield borrowed some existing folk tunes, and could well have borrowed the 'Auld Lang Syne' tune from the same source as did Burns.

All the above ancestors of the 'Auld Lang Syne' tune were instrumental, intended to accompany the Scottish dance form called a strathspey. So

Robbie Burns.

within the practice of the times, Burns was not being a plagiarist to use and polish a fiddle solo and combine it with words. On the contrary, it took his genius to wed two non-related fragments – one musical, the other an attractive dialect expression – into a form which much of the world now recognises and loves. Several centuries have passed since 'Apollo's Banquet' was last performed but 'Auld Lang Syne' is sung often. Curiously, Burns' five-verse 'Auld Lang Syne' was not published until 1796, after the poet's death. 'Auld Lang Syne' is described by Scottish writers as a dismissory song, one associated with leave-taking. Presumably it functions in this way at New Year's Eve because it is farewelling one year to prepare for the next. Some European countries associate its leave-taking more directly, as a song farewelling people on their way somewhere.

American musician Guy Lombardo recalled 'Auld Lang Syne' being sung by Scottish immigrants in Canada when he was a boy in the early 1900s. Later in New York, when he formed his band the Royal Canadians, Lombardo arranged the song and put it in the band's repertoire. In 1929 they played the number in a radio broadcast on New Year's Eve, and a tradition was born. For the next 40 years, America heard Guy Lombardo and his band on radio, and then television, play 'Auld Lang Syne' every 31 December. Lombardo was so closely associated with the song that many people thought he was its composer.

There is no exact list of how many times 'Auld Lang Syne' has been recorded, but the total is believed to be over 1000, including some rather unexpected versions. As an instrumental, the song can be heard as a harp solo by Bronn Journey; or played by the Washington Saxophone Quartet; and performed on electric power tools by Woody Philips. Jimi Hendrix recorded a version, as did the Barenaked Ladies, and the Beach Boys. Several dance versions are available, including disco and polka. In 2000, British pop star Cliff Richard had a No. 1 hit when he recorded 'The Lord's Prayer' to the tune of 'Auld Lang Syne'.

Excluding recordings, it would not be possible to estimate the number of times the song has been sung. John Cairney, himself a renowned performer of Burns' works, invariably asked his audiences to hum the tune, while he recited the words of all the verses. The tune has also emerged in some unexpected places. Starting in 1896, the 'national song' of Korea was sung to the tune of 'Auld Lang Syne', until the invasion by Japan in 1910 banned its use. The melody can also be heard in Taiwan at funerals and, curiously, at Taiwanese graduation ceremonies. India presents the tune as part of military passing-out ceremonies, and crowds in Thailand sing it after sports matches. In the Philippines the citizens sing it not just for New Year, but also for Christmas Day.

Among English-speaking people in modern times, and in a non-Scottish context, some of the original words have become modified, usually to make them easier to sing and to understand. John Cairney notes that usage has replaced Burns' 'my jo' with 'my friend' or 'my dear' and that sometimes the 'cup of kindness' becomes a 'kiss of kindness'. He also points out that the correct 's' sound for 'syne' is often replaced by the harder 'z'.

The original version of 'Auld Lang Syne', as written by Robert Burns:

Should auld acquaintance be forgot
And never brought to mind?
Should auld acquaintance be forgot
And days o lang syne?
Chorus
For auld lang syne, my jo
For auld lang syne
We'll tak a cup of kindness yet,
For auld lang syne.

And surely you'll be your pint-stowp,
And surely I'll be mine,
And we'll tak a cup o kindness yet
For auld lang syne!
Chorus

We twa hae run abott the braes
And pu'd the gowans fine,
And we've wander'd mony a fit,
Sin auld lang syne.
Chorus

41

We twa hae paidl'd in the burn
Frae morning sun till dine
But seas between us baith hae roar'd
Sin auld lang syne.
Chorus

And there's a hand, my trusty fiere
And gie's a hand o thine
And we'll tak a right guid-willie waught
For auld lang syne.
Chorus

Dr Cairney gives a glossary for international understanding:

my jo – close friend, companion, partner

pint-stowp – a drink container made from tin, holding half a gallon (just over a litre). The suggestion is that only a man in extreme poverty would not be able to afford one drink for himself, and to provide one other for his friend

twa – two

aboot the braes – about the hills

pu'd the gowans – picked the daisies

wander'd mony a fit – to walk a long way on foot

paidl'd in the burn – paddled in a small stream

dine – the 'dinner' meal, which could be either at noon or night

sin – not sin, but abbreviation of 'since'

fiere – a word arising from spinning flax, which came to mean the judging by which a friendship is measured, a 'standard-bearer'

guid-willie – goodwill

waught – a drink

Hello, Dolly!

It's so nice to have you back where you belong.

JERRY HERMAN, 1963

In spite of her somewhat raucous persona, Dolly Levi's original heritage was from the very top drawer of the arcane British literary élite: the story that eventually gave the world 'Hello, Dolly!' began in 19th-century London.

John Oxenford (1812–77) was articled as a solicitor and experienced in financial and commercial legal matters. An ardent reader and impressive linguist, he translated Goethe's *Autobiography* from the German, Molière's *Tartuffe* from French and Boyardo's *Orlando Innamorato* from Italian. His essay on the philosophy of Schopenhauer helped establish that scholar's fame in English-speaking countries. Oxenford was also much interested in drama and became a drama critic for *The Times*, besides writing over 60 plays himself.

One of these, in 1835, was a light, fast-moving farce called *A Day Well Spent*. Its core story was about two young men apprentices who set out for an adventure in the city, hoping that their rich but miserly employer would never find out. Sound familiar? Perhaps, but there was still quite a way to go before getting to the Harmonia Gardens.

Oxenford's play was noticed by Austrian playwright Johann Nestroy, known in his homeland as 'the king of comedy'. The result, in 1842, was *Einen Jux will er sich machen* ('He's out for a good time'), which played in Vienna. Oxenford's original and Nestroy's version may well have remained in the European repertoire forever as period pieces, and indeed they did so for over 90 years. Then, in 1938, the play came to the attention of the distinguished American writer, Thornton Wilder.

Although attracted to the play, Wilder knew better than just to 'adapt' an existing

English–Viennese comedy: he needed to restructure it. So the action was moved to the fringe of New York, and the emphasis shifted onto the employer, who became the title role, *The Merchant of Yonkers*. And most importantly, a new character was added.

Since American women had been given the vote just over a decade before, some changes were emerging in the gender balance. Possibly aware of this, Wilder created the character of a strong woman who linked the existing plot strands of the curmudgeonly employer with an eye on marriage, and the two young men with an eye on adventure. In the person of popular actress Jane Cowl, audiences first met Dolly Levi.

Alas, in spite of the successful track record of its two predecessor plays, and in spite of its talented and popular cast, *The Merchant of Yonkers* failed to cut it with New York audiences, and came off after only 39 performances. Dolly was put on a shelf.

There she gathered dust for 15 years, until British director Tyrone Guthrie took an interest, and suggested a restaging of *The Merchant of Yonkers*. Unhappy about the play's fate in 1938, Wilder had to be persuaded into agreement – but only with a rewrite. The revised version shifted the emphasis further onto the one-woman dating service known as Dolly Levi, and expanded that role considerably. *The Matchmaker*, starring Ruth Gordon, opened in 1954 at the Edinburgh Festival where it was a great success, later transferring to London. American seasons followed in Philadelphia and Boston, building up impetus for the big one, a Broadway opening in 1955. Dolly Levi was back in New York.

Wilder was well educated in traditional European drama, and his restructured script for *The Matchmaker* drew on successful theatrical traditions that reached back to ancient Rome. There, and in succeeding centuries, a bumbling servant was a frequent dramatic character, as were innocent maidens, a brassy harridan and a miser. In 200 BC Plautus had created the template of the wealthy skinflint, which resurfaced in many different guises in the following centuries: Shakespeare's *A Comedy of Errors*, Molière's *Le Misanthrope*, Dickens' *A Christmas Carol*, even Scrooge McDuck. And Molière's miser character of 1668 employed the services of an arranger-of-dates, one Frosine, who was the direct ancestor of Wilder's Dolly Levi. It is often noted that Dolly's speech, persuading the miserly Vandergelder of a young woman's charms, is more than reminiscent of Frosine's speech with the same purpose, written 286 years before: 'She is a girl accustomed to cheese, milk, salad and apples – she will not expect an elaborate table or rich soups. This is not of small importance, and could be a saving of several thousand francs a year. Besides this, she does not want expensive gowns and elaborate and costly decorations.' And so Frosine/Dolly continues, bamboozling the miser with dodgy logic which he finds it difficult to displace.

Wilder's *Matchmaker* was a major stage hit in Britain, the United States and the Continent, and was filmed with Shirley Booth in the title role. A decade after the play's opening, plans were being discussed for yet another major incarnation, as a musical.

Composer Jerry Herman, still in his early 30s, heard on the grapevine that David Merrick was planning this musical and was keen to be involved. He arranged an appointment with Merrick and auditioned himself by sitting down and playing four songs of his own composition. According to legend, Merrick turned to the young man and said, 'Kid, the show is yours.'

The musical *Hello, Dolly!* was the fifth reincarnation of John Oxenford's original play. Early in its genesis, the musical had several changes of name, but settled on *Hello, Dolly!*, which had its first performances in Detroit in 1963 to a somewhat lacklustre response. There was a strong possibility that Dolly Levi would return to the dusty shelf where she had already spent many years. But no. With some gentle readjusting, *Hello, Dolly!* opened in New York in January 1964 and entered theatrical and musical history. In the person of Carol Channing, the glorious, zany, flamboyant character of Dolly Levi became the stuff of legend. The New York production earned 10 Tony Awards and the New York Drama Critics' Circle Award for Best Comedy of the 1963–64 season.

At the core of the musical was the title song, a simple bouncy little number which, with clever orchestration and brilliant staging, became the focal point of the show. Musical analysts pointed out that the song did not actually advance the action of the story at all, and Dolly Levi's coming back to a restaurant from which she had been absent for a while might not seem sufficient for a full-scale song and dance number, but this one virtually stopped the show. The bizarre theatricality of it all – the befeathered diva swathed in scarlet, progressing down a staircase surrounded by a bevy of waiters dancing complex restaurant moves with split-second energy – captured every audience who saw it. New York critic Walter Kerr described it as 'the best single piece of sheer musical comedy staging I have ever seen'. Along with Kerr, 2844 other audiences saw *Hello, Dolly!* performances on Broadway, and there were thousands of other performances throughout the world.

Carol Channing, the original singing Dolly, was eventually replaced by Ginger

Rogers and then an impressive parade of stellar women, no longer young (as suited the role), played Dolly: Mary Martin, Betty Grable, Martha Raye, Phyllis Diller, Ethel Merman, Dorothy Lamour, Eve Arden and Pearl Bailey (heading an all-black cast).

In spite of being described by the cynical as a 'hymn to the menopause', the magic of 'Hello, Dolly!' captured most of the planet. Within a short time of the show's opening, it was estimated that 90 artists had recorded the title song.

But there was a glitch. Composer Mack David listened to the song and promptly sued Jerry Herman for infringement of copyright. The first four bars of the 'Hello, Dolly!' tune were almost an exact replica of David's 1948 song, 'Sunflower' ('She's a sunflower, she's my one flower, she's the flower of my heart'). Although Jerry Herman

claimed later that he had never heard the song – he was only 16 in 1948 – he could see that the situation was potentially serious: a trial could affect the show itself, and the possible movie that was being mentioned. Reluctantly, he agreed to settle out of court for a sum that was rumoured to be $250,000.

Of the many recordings made of 'Hello, Dolly!', by far the most popular was that of famous trumpeter Louis Armstrong. His singing voice resembled a handful of stones being rolled in a barrel, but those particular stones in that particular barrel combined to make a sound of irresistible charm.

Armstrong's famous recording was made in New York in December 1963, before the show had even opened in New York.

In 1963 Carol Channing premiered the new musical Hello, Dolly! *in Detroit.*

Armstrong's bass player Arvell Shaw recounted to jazz archivist Ken Burns that after the December recording session, the band went on tour through Europe. As the tour progressed, audiences started calling out for 'Hello, Dolly!', but by then Satchmo, as he was known, had forgotten both the tune and the words, which had to be sent to him from New York so he could accommodate the requests. Armstrong's recording of 'Hello, Dolly!' sold several million and became the No. 1 pop hit in the United States for 1964, dislodging the Beatles. Moves began to write Louis Armstrong into the forthcoming *Hello, Dolly!* film.

The movie was the next adaptation, and that word is used deliberately, since many who had enjoyed the role of Dolly being played by 'mature' favourites of stage and screen, found it a shock that the role on screen was to be played by 26-year-old Barbra Streisand. That she was feisty and could sing there was no doubt, but to play a grieving middle-aged widow she was a curious choice. One of the movie's high points came when Louis Armstrong joined Streisand in 'Hello, Dolly!', amid the extraordinary splendour of Hollywood's version of New York's Harmonia Gardens.

But curiously, adaptations of that long-ago little play *A Day Well Spent* weren't yet finished. In 1981, playwright Tom Stoppard drew on Nestroy's Viennese version of Oxenford's original English play for *On the Razzle*, which retained Nestroy's Viennese setting and period, but was now presented with English dialogue redolent with Stoppard wit. So since 1835, the basic story has had six different theatrical adaptations, but since 1963 Jerry Herman's song 'Hello, Dolly!' has provided the magic that brought the old British story to life.

Lili Marlene

Underneath the lamplight,
By the barrack gate.

HANS LEIP, NORBERT SCHULTZE, 1937

If all the women who claimed to have had romantic liaisons with German soldier-poet Hans Leip were telling the truth, he would have had no time for sentry duty. All the women, invariably, claimed that they were the original inspiration for Leip's poem, 'The Song of a Young Sentry', which later became a real song, 'Lili Marlene'. But the women's claims were fanciful, for Lili Marlene was never one person but a combination of two.

In 1915, aged 22, as a soldier fighting in the First World War, Hans Leip wrote his poem to express the anguish of separation from his sweetheart, a grocer's daughter named Lili. On sentry duty at night, he would receive a friendly wave from a nurse going off duty; her name was Marleen. In 1937, feeling that the darkness of another war was looming, Leip released his collection of poems, including 'The Song of a Young Sentry', under the title *Die Hafenorgel* (The Little Organ by the Harbour). It was his hope that those who had not lived through the First World War might be alerted to the pain, horror and death of wars fought in the name of so-called 'national pride'.

By then, his 'Young Sentry' poem had been set to music by a composer called Rudolf Zink and it was sung by cabaret artist Eulalie Bunnenberg, then known as Liselott Wilke. But Zink's melody vanished without trace after Leip's poem was published in 1937. Then a new tune was penned for the poem.

Norbert Schultze was a very successful German composer of songs, opera and movie music. He barely remembered the Great War but when he read Leip's poems, he immediately caught their ominous connotations and produced a new melody for the

'Young Sentry' poem. But in spite of Schultze's track record as a successful composer, the new song was rejected by several publishers. To some the tune seemed wistful; to others it was mournful. To some it was a lilting melody; to others, the tune was not solemn enough for the sadness of the subject. By 1939 Schultze had modified the composition so that it was ready for publication and for recording. By that time the former Liselott Wilke, now a very successful singer under the name Lale Andersen, was offered the new song to record. It didn't appeal to her at all but she did make the recording, just before the outbreak of the Second World War. The recording made little impact and its sales were lacklustre. More seriously, machinations motivated by Nazi politics nearly sent the song into permanent oblivion.

Joseph Goebbels, Adolf Hitler's propaganda chief, was reported as hating the song for not being 'military' enough. He proclaimed that its melody should be changed into a stirring march. To loyalist Nazis, the song seemed to be anti-war, possibly even close to treason, and singer Lale Andersen was believed to be sympathetic towards Jews. The song was banned and both Andersen and Schultze were charged with 'moral sabotage' of the nation's aims. She was placed virtually under house arrest and he was ordered to compose music praising Nazi ideals.

By 1941, when Germany was 'occupying' Yugoslavia, the Germans were broadcasting to their troops in North Africa from a radio station in Belgrade. When the station was shelled, most of its records were smashed and the station was desperately short of music to play. One day the station's military director, Lieutenant Karl-Heinz Reintgen, came across a dusty box in which a few records had survived – and right at the bottom was 'Lili Marleen'. Officially the recording had been banned, but Reintgen knew that a buddy of his in the Afrika Korps had quite liked the song, and they had precious little else to play, so 'Lili Marleen' was broadcast.

It was a turning point. The German troops asked for the recording over and over again, and non-military people who could hear the station also requested it. To the surprise, and horror, of the Nazi high command, 'Lili Marleen' gained a following that seemed unstoppable. Even Germany's enemies somehow obtained Lale Andersen's recording, and far from being banned, her voice was being heard across Europe singing the sad strains about Lili under the lamplight.

Field Marshal Erwin Rommel didn't agree with Goebbels and asked Radio Belgrade to play the song every night before closing down at 10 p.m. 'Lili Marleen' quickly became virtually the anthem of the Afrika Korps, and Goebbels was forced to retract, and to pretend that the Nazis welcomed the song. Norbert Schultze and Lale Andersen were brought in from the cold, and both were sent around Germany to perform the song.

Some songs generated by war are jaunty and confidence-boosting, often scorning the enemy. Others are redolent with hope and vision of a conflict-free future, or reminisce about happier times in a more innocent past. 'Lili Marleen' did not fall clearly into any category, but the tune, even without its words, had a haunting appeal, as was soon to be proven. Allied troops in Africa could also hear the German broadcasts, and the plaintive song rapidly crossed enemy lines and soon became an immense favourite with the Eighth Army, who sang it with its original German words, and then the American troops followed suit.

When a group of British soldiers were on leave in London, publisher Jimmy Phillips chided them for singing a German song in German, so the men promptly challenged him to produce an English version. Phillips did so, in collaboration with Tommy Connor. Their 'translation', along with the differing versions now available in Germany, offered words which differed somewhat from Leip's original poem. Although still plaintive, it was now a bitter-sweet song of dreaming about a distant love, rather than a plangent anti-war statement. And Lili's name was gently anglicised to Marlene.

Anne Shelton recorded this English version with the Ambrose Orchestra, and the BBC promoted it enthusiastically, establishing its popularity throughout Britain. In France, Suzy Solidor recorded it in French. By 1943 German-born anti-Nazi Marlene Dietrich was singing the song throughout war-torn Europe, and continued to sing it throughout the rest of her career, as did Vera Lynn. Many recordings followed – Bing Crosby, Edith Piaf, Perry Como and Jean Claude Pascal.

Hans Leip died in 1983, and the tune's composer Norbert Schultze in 2002. They had seen their song survive the Second World War, be translated into 48 languages (including Hebrew and Latin) and feature on hit parades in countries as diverse as the United States and Japan. When the original recording artist, Lale Anderson, was asked in 1972 if she could explain the popularity of 'Lili Marlene', she replied, 'Can the wind explain why it became a storm?'

Somewhere Over the Rainbow

There's a land that I heard of.

HAROLD ARLEN, YIP HARBURG, 1939

In 1898, when American author Frank Baum was writing his story about a girl named Dorothy being transported to a magical land, he could not think of a name for her destination. One day, when looking at his two-drawer filing cabinet, he noticed the top drawer was labelled A–N, and the bottom drawer was labelled O–Z. Suddenly, the magic land had a name, Oz.

Lyman Frank Baum was born in 1856 and as a teenager began his own newspaper, which later grew into a magazine. Although his family background was wealthy, young Frank had a somewhat wayward employment history – actor, store manager, reporter and travelling salesman for crockery and axle grease. When he was married and had become father to four sons, Baum delighted in telling fanciful stories to his children and their friends. In 1897 he got round to writing his first book, *Mother Goose in Prose*, and it was a huge success, followed soon by *Father Goose: His Book*, which became a bestseller in 1899.

His fanciful stories for his children and neighbours usually included whimsical characters who lived in a fantasy land. Baum's mother-in-law persuaded him that these stories and the fantasy land should be put into his next book so, with the help of the filing cabinet title, *The Wonderful Wizard of Oz* came into being in 1900. The book was an overnight success, establishing Baum as the foremost children's author of the day. The first stage show of *The Wizard of Oz* appeared two years after Baum's book was published, and played seasons in Chicago and Broadway during 1902–03, then toured the United States until 1911.

Eventually, Baum wrote 14 more books about Oz. Two were made into silent movies without causing much impact; the 1925 version featured a young Oliver Hardy as the Tin Man. But the books were making an impact: by 1938, a staggering 10 million copies had been sold.

Aware of the success of Walt Disney's *Snow White and the Seven Dwarfs*, MGM acquired the screen rights to *The Wizard of Oz*, and 16-year-old Judy Garland, on a singing tour in Pennsylvania, read an announcement in a magazine that she was to play Dorothy. The administrative brass of the studio had originally wanted Shirley Temple, whose presence on screen was pure gold at the box office, but whose singing voice, although charming, was a little threadbare.

There was concern about which type of music would suit the Oz story – Classical? Ballads? Swing? Semi-operatic? (Sopranos Jeanette MacDonald and Deanna Durbin were both enjoying great public success.) Finally it was decided that standard melodies of a popular accessible kind, without gimmicks, would best suit the story, and its star. Harold Arlen and E.Y. ('Yip') Harburg were contracted to do the composing. They worked well together, but after completing 45 minutes of music for the film, they were still missing one vital thing – Dorothy's solo, to be sung by Judy Garland.

Inspiration was slow in coming. One day when Harold Arlen and his wife were out driving, he suddenly asked her to stop the car and there, outside a pharmacy, he took out a piece of manuscript paper and began writing a tune that would become Dorothy's song. Now it needed lyrics. The song needed to show that Dorothy was a troubled little girl in Kansas and Yip Harburg considered her childhood was colourless; in Baum's original novel, the word 'grey' occurs nine times in three pages when referring to the drought in the state. He pictured her in a countryside which was dry, dusty and arid, with almost no flowers and although Baum's book never mentioned it, he mused that one of the few coloured things Dorothy might ever have seen in nature was a rainbow. Harburg and Arlen began referring to the still non-existent song by a temporary title, 'I Want to Get on the Other Side of the Rainbow'.

Initially, Harburg found Arlen's music for the song somewhat grand, with suggestions of religious hymns and Pachelbel's 'Canon'. He pointed out that the character was a 12-year-old girl, not an opera singer, so Arlen reduced the rather dramatic accompaniment. Harburg was also concerned about the melody's opening octave leap. How to fit that with the sound of a young character, and make it sound logical? But Harburg had written the words for 'Brother, Can You Spare a Dime?', and he understood poverty and the Depression. Over the next three weeks he found himself unable to escape from his initial rainbow image, but had difficulty fitting that to Arlen's tune. Eventually he tried singing the melody with just open vowels. 'Aa-aa' didn't suggest anything; neither did 'Ee-ee'. But when he got to 'Oh-oh' 'the other side' fell into place as 'somewhere over'. The journey towards the complete song had begun.

In a brave move, it was decided that the Kansas scenes, including Dorothy's song, would be filmed in sepia tones, which would burst into colour when she arrived in Oz. In film terms, there were problems galore. The new technique of Technicolor was still uncertain and at first the Yellow Brick Road photographed as green; Buddy Ebsen as the Tin Man became so ill with the aluminium powder that he nearly died and had to be replaced; Margaret Hamilton, playing the Wicked Witch of the West, 'disappeared' into a fire effect that burned her so badly she couldn't appear for another six weeks.

The *Wizard of Oz* movie employed a combination of 14 writers and five directors, who between them turned Baum's concept of Oz into a screenplay. In the process, Dorothy's slippers which, according to Baum, were silver, were changed to ruby, and the fantasy characters played 'double' roles as workers on the Kansas farm. The first of the directors, Richard Thorpe, attempted to make Judy Garland glamorous. She was wigged into shoulder-length blonde ringlets, and given arched eyebrows and bee-stung red lips to make her look cute. It didn't look right. Thorpe was relieved of his duties, and replaced temporarily by George Cukor, who immediately abandoned all the artificiality and reshot all Garland's footage, now with her own innocent fresh face and her own hair in bunches. Then Victor Fleming took over, but had to leave to work on *Gone With the Wind*.

The next director, King Vidor, put his stamp on 'Somewhere Over the Rainbow'. Having had experience in silent movies, he knew that movements and context help tell a story as much as words. Dreaming of her land over the rainbow, Dorothy should not just stand and sing: rather, audiences should see the contrast between where she was and where she wanted to be. So Garland sang the wistful song in a barnyard, seen against

Film historians believe they can point to the *Wizard's* influence on later movie-making. *Star Wars*, for example, features a hairy man and a tin man, and includes fights with and against the forces of magic. *E.T.* may also have been inspired by the Oz story, but in an inverted form. Instead of a normal child being transported to a fantasy land and wanting to go home, *E.T.* is a fantasy person transported to a 'normal' universe and wanting to go home.

a fence, a haystack and a harvester. Yip Harburg's son later reported that neither his father nor Harold Arlen was prepared for the effect when Judy Garland first sang the song on the film set and its magic began to work.

Twice cut from the movie, eventually Judy Garland's song was allowed to remain – and she sang it for the rest of her life.

In hindsight it seems hard to credit, but after the movie's preview 'Somewhere Over the Rainbow' was removed. MGM executives decreed that it was too long, it slowed down the action, and it was not dignified for an MGM star to be seen wandering in a barnyard accompanied by hens, a haystack, livestock, rusty machinery and a nondescript little dog. The song was then restored, then removed again. But finally, good sense prevailed and the song was restored once more. To anyone now familiar with *The Wizard Of Oz*, the decision to cut 'Somewhere Over the Rainbow' seems rather like removing the Eiffel Tower from Paris. The purpose and meaning of the whole story revolves around the yearning that Dorothy feels.

The song's reinstatement was justified in the best way possible, at the 1940 Academy Awards, when Arlen and Harburg won the Oscar for best song. Then Mickey Rooney announced that the Oscar for outstanding performance by a juvenile actress over the past year went to Judy Garland. At the after-Oscar ball, the song most requested of the band was 'Somewhere Over the Rainbow'.

In spite of these credentials and its very large expenditure, in its early years *The Wizard of Oz* was popular but not a financial blockbuster. Cinemas were consistently full, but usually with children, at half price, which did not add up to big takings. But in 1956, its first screening on CBS American television completely changed the movie's status and popularity. With only a minimal choice of channels at the time, *The Wizard of Oz* gained a huge number of viewers and became a major talking point, even though it was seen in black and white. It was considered that another showing too soon would be a risk, so the second showing was held back until 1959 when the viewing numbers broke all records. Showings were then scheduled for once a year, and the numbers of viewers continued to grow. The arrival of colour television provided another boost, and huge audiences saw the movie, which was now over 20 years old.

Central to the movie's core and message was 'Somewhere Over the Rainbow'. Seemingly a trifle sung by a teenager, it had a subtle depth and strength that struck a resonant chord in the hearts of Americans, and then gradually throughout the world. Judy Garland's extraordinary capacity to convey belief in lyrics meant listeners heard in the song their own dreams and aspirations.

In Dorothy's journey to the other side of her rainbow there were echoes of a thousand brave adventurous travels, from ancient Greek classics through to modern science fiction. People everywhere could identify with the girl whose life was 'grey' and who dreamed of a distant life where dreams came true. And yet there was also a comforting hint of realism in Dorothy's story. She was Cinderella in reverse: the girl who went to a vivid Technicolor ball but when she got home realised that home was best.

Besides the 1902 stage musical, the story has since surfaced in several other stage versions, including a landmark presentation in Britain by the Royal Shakespeare Company in 1987. By then a version called *The Wiz*, adapted for black American performers, had opened on Broadway in 1975 and ran for four years; it was made into a film starring Diana Ross and Michael Jackson, Lena Horne and Richard Pryor. A 2003 musical, *Wicked*, was derived from a Baum spin-off by Gregory Maguire containing elements of the original story, without being an exact presentation of *The Wizard Of Oz*.

'I'm Always Chasing Rainbows' is credited to Harry Carroll and Joseph McCarthy but the tune is actually by Chopin: 'Fantasie Impromptu in C sharp minor'. 'Full Moon and Empty Arms', as 'composed' by Buddy Kaye and Ted Mossman, owes its melody to Sergei Rachmaninov's second piano concerto.

When L. Frank Baum died in 1919 he had written a total of 60 books, including those about the adventures in Oz. Other authors continued to write about Oz until eventually there were 40 books. But the 1939 movie still stands as the supreme telling of Baum's story, and as one of the supreme movies of all time. And the melody of 'Somewhere Over the Rainbow' is an inextricable part of that supremacy.

Some years later, Judy Garland wrote to Harold Arlen that 'Somewhere Over the Rainbow' had 'become part of my life. I have sung it thousands of times, and it is still the song closest to my heart.' Sadly, in her own life, Garland never seemed to find the place where troubles melt like lemon drops. In March 1969 she gave a concert at the Falkoner Centre in Copenhagen, and closed the performance with 'Somewhere Over the Rainbow'. The audience stood and cheered, and an attendant came forward to present her with flowers shaped like a rainbow. Nobody knew that Judy Garland would never sing again. For 30 years she had told the world about a land she'd heard of once in a lullaby. Three months after that Copenhagen performance, the lullaby ended, but the song remained a legacy for those still able to hope.

Yesterday

All my troubles seemed so far away.

JOHN LENNON, PAUL McCARTNEY, 1965

A number of authors and artists have acknowledged that their successful works were inspired by dreams – Robert Louis Stevenson's *The Strange Case of Dr Jekyll and Mr Hyde*, Mary Shelley's *Frankenstein*, Samuel Taylor Coleridge's *Kubla Khan* and some of the graphic output of Salvador Dali and William Blake. But inspiration from a dream is more rare in music. The legendary 'Devil's Trill' violin sonata was, somewhat apocryphally, claimed by composer Giuseppe Tartini to have been brought to him in 1765 by the devil himself, in a dream. One of the Beatles' most popular songs came by the same method, though not via the devil.

The entire tune of the song 'Yesterday' came to former Beatle Paul McCartney in 1965 when he was asleep and upon waking he immediately turned on a tape recorder and played the melody on a keyboard. At first he was concerned that he had simply recalled something he'd already heard, but when he asked around nobody recognised it.

But lyrics were needed. Initially the only words that crossed McCartney's mind in response to the rhythm of the dreamt melody were 'Scrambled eggs, oh my baby how I love your legs'. Somehow that didn't seem right. McCartney went on holiday to Portugal and came back with a new set of words that were to become world famous.

This was 1965, Paul McCartney was 22 and the Beatles had already become an incredible phenomenon, though their fame would increase. Tumultuous crowds, screaming girls, booming record sales and blanket press coverage were a fact of daily life for the four young men. They had appeared in the 1963 Royal Variety show, alongside Sophie Tucker, Maurice Chevalier and movie star Marlene Dietrich. At first sight, Miss Dietrich, not knowing who the Beatles were, did not take kindly to the mop-tops. Her daughter later reported that Dietrich said, 'What are those? They look like monkeys with all that hair. All this big security and *they* got in – how terrible!' It was explained to Dietrich that the Beatles were a new rage and adored by the youth audience. It was also suggested to her that it would create a stir if she were to be photographed with them. Dietrich was reluctant, but allowed a message to be sent to the Fab Four that she would like to meet them.

The resulting photo was published all over the world: the Legend and the soon-to-become-legends. And the telecast of the show was seen by an estimated 26,000,000 viewers, which helped cause a distinct change in Marlene Dietrich's attitude. She announced to her daughter and anyone else who would listen: 'I asked them for autographs for my grandchildren – and they said all they wanted was a picture taken with me! So of course I said yes. They are geniuses!'

Most of the Beatles' repertoire was composed within the group; they rarely sang other composers' material. Initially music critics didn't take them seriously, but this attitude later changed. Beatles biographer Geoffrey Stokes quoted *The Times* music critic, who found their music 'expressively unusual and harmonically intriguing'. He may have been a little carried away when he continued: 'chains of pandiatonic clusters, and major tonic sevenths and ninths and flat submediant key switches, so natural in the aeolian cadence at the end of "Not a Second Time" (the chord progression that ends Mahler's "Song of the Earth").' Undeterred by such sober, and often obscure, analysis, the Beatles continued in their own way, sometimes with deliberate musical antics. Their 1964 No. 1 hit single 'I Feel Fine' began with guitar feedback and finished with barking dogs.

'Yesterday' was recorded in June 1965 at the EMI studios in Abbey Road. To begin with,

Several publishers said no to the first Harry Potter novel. The young Maria Callas once came second in a talent quest (whatever happened to the winner?), Decca turned down the young Beatles. To these examples of opportunity-eccentrics can be added British singer Billy J. Kramer. In 1965 he asked Paul McCartney if he had any new song which he, Kramer, could record. McCartney said yes, played him an early version of 'Yesterday' and asked if he would like to record it. Kramer said no. His judgement wasn't echoed by over 1000 other recording artists, and listeners in their millions. But Kramer wasn't a total loser: having turned down 'Yesterday' he instead recorded a version of 'Little Children', which became one his most popular hits.

the four men played their guitars and drums as McCartney sang, but that didn't sound right. John Lennon experimented with adding an organ part, but that didn't work either. Producer George Martin's suggestion of a string section wasn't welcomed; they didn't want to sound like Mantovani. Eventually, McCartney recorded the track singing solo, accompanying himself on the Epiphone Gibson Texan acoustic guitar he'd bought the year before. He finished recording the track in only two takes. And Martin persuaded McCartney to accept an overdub by an austere string quartet. Suddenly, the plaintive solo-voice-with-guitar gained a slightly richer and more sophisticated sound, its sadness was somehow enhanced and one of the most successful recording tracks in history was completed.

But there were still problems.

McCartney's appearance on the track as a solo artist caused unrest within the group. All their recordings so far had been as an ensemble, without highlighting any individual member. Furthermore, the song's simplicity was somewhat distant from the insouciance that had become the Beatles' trademark. This song was definitely not rock'n'roll, it was uncharacteristic of their offerings so far and the three non-participants joined to block any issue of 'Yesterday' as a single in Britain. (It was released initially as part of the *Help* album.)

Musicologists often commented on the complexity of the Beatles' music – their use of subdominants, descending chromatics and plagal cadences. It's doubtful Paul McCartney understood such terms since he couldn't read music. 'Yesterday' did not contain all the complexities attributed to the Beatles, but McCartney's impressive natural musicianship produced a song with a confident and satisfying structure. One unusual feature is that the opening phrase is only seven bars long, instead of the traditional and usual eight bars. Before 'Yesterday', Paul McCartney's contributions had been jaunty, and John Lennon was considered the source of more reflective material. Beatle-composed songs were all credited to Lennon and McCartney, as was 'Yesterday', but this one was McCartney's work alone.

McCartney also used 'Yesterday' in his own defence. A couple of years before its release, the mother of a former girlfriend had accused him of having no feelings. In August 1965 McCartney phoned her and said, 'You know that you said I had no feelings? Watch TV on Sunday then tell me I've got no feelings.' The following Sunday, the Beatles appeared on BBC's *Blackpool Night Out* and performed 'Yesterday' live for the first time.

The success of 'Yesterday' had the force of a tsunami. It received so many awards that no one house could hold them. The song had, and still has, universal appeal. Everyday words, in almost-spoken rhythm, are married seamlessly to an endearing tune. It is a rare person who cannot identify with its lament for lost love. Analysts wonder how McCartney could present such a plaintive view when he was only 22, and hardly suffering from lost love. He was living with his girlfriend Jane Asher when he initially dreamed the tune and then wrote the words.

The earlier possibility, that McCartney had somehow inadvertently 'remembered' a tune, rather than dreamed it, surfaced again on at least three occasions. Music writers suggested that the tune of 'Yesterday' sounded suspiciously like the song ' Answer Me', as recorded by Nat King Cole 11 years earlier. And another carping drew comparisons with Ray Charles' version of 'Georgia on My Mind'. The most bizarre claim came 40 years after McCartney recorded 'Yesterday', when an Italian musician claimed that the melody was a direct steal from 'Piccere Che Vene a Dicere', a Neapolitan song composed in 1895. The bother didn't last long: nobody seemed able to produce evidence that the Neapolitan song existed on record, which McCartney might or might not have heard, or had been published as sheet music, which he couldn't read. Each claim caused only a brief flutter, submerged by the overwhelming acceptance and popularity of McCartney's song.

'Yesterday' became one of the most-recorded pieces of music in history. It has

Paul McCartney in 1965, the year of 'Yesterday'.

been played as jazz, reggae, salsa, soul, funk and folk, by brass, synthesiser, harmonica and symphony orchestra. The *Guinness Book of Records* notes that within a year of its release, over 1500 cover versions of 'Yesterday' had been recorded. Among the artists who have recorded the song are Elvis Presley, Benny Goodman, Michael Bolton, the Ray Conniff Singers, Bobby Goldsboro, Joan Baez, Acker Bilk, Liberace, Kenneth McKellar, Nana Mouskouri, Ray Charles, Placido Domingo, Marianne Faithful, Marvin Gaye and Frank Sinatra – to name but a few. In 1999, Broadcast Music Incorporated (an organisation monitoring copyright clearances and performing royalty payments) estimated that 'Yesterday' had been played on radio approximately seven million times during the 20th century.

Since John Lennon had in fact not contributed to the song's composition or performance, 35 years after its release, McCartney attempted to redress the ascribed 'composed by' from Lennon and McCartney, to McCartney and Lennon, but was unsuccessful.

'Yesterday', performed by McCartney, surfaced in the film *Give My Regards to Broad Street* in 1984. McCartney had filmed the sequence the year before, standing on a London street dressed in grubby clothes singing with his guitar, while being secretly filmed from a nearby closed van. None of the public recognised the semi-derelict middle-aged busker, and the £2.40 that sympathetic passers-by dropped into his hat was donated to the Seamen's Mission.

In 1979 Leonard Bernstein, asked by *Rolling Stone* to write about the Beatles, admitted to having fallen in love with their music, describing the 'frabjous falsetto-cum-croon, the ineluctable beat, the flawless intonation, the utterly fresh lyrics, the Schubert-like flow of musical invention, and the f--- you coolness of these Four Horsemen of Our Apocalypse'.

Bernstein wasn't the only classical musician to applaud Beatles music. Famed British composer John Rutter

Intrigued by the bourrée from J.S. Bach's Suite in E minor, Paul McCartney and George Harrison adapted it into the Beatles hit, 'Blackbird'.

created 'The Beatles Concerto', featuring the melody of 'Yesterday', recorded by the full Royal Philharmonic conducted by Ron Goodwin, with pianists Peter Rostal and Paul Schaefer. So far, it is said to be the only time in history a No.1 pop hit has been heard in a piano concerto.

White Christmas

Where the tree-tops glisten
And children listen.

IRVING BERLIN, 1940

As a child Israel Beilin would certainly have known white December snows in the little Russian town where he was born in 1888. They would not have been associated with Christmas, however; the family was Jewish and Israel's father Moishe was a cantor in the local synagogue. Yet young Israel later created America's most popular Christmas song.

As oppression of Jews and raids by Cossacks became a real danger, the Beilin family – parents and six children – made an arduous and secret journey to Belgium. Once there, they managed to sail to the United States. The family arrived in New York in 1893, and were registered as Baline. The youngest child, now called Izzy Baline, endured grinding poverty during the next few years. When his father died three years later, Izzy helped to support his family by busking, singing in the streets and sometimes in not very salubrious bars. Eventually he became a singing waiter in a Chinatown café.

When he was 18 his first song lyrics, with music by Nick Nicholson, were published. By then Israel Beilin had morphed from Izzy Baline into Irving Berlin. This song, 'Marie From Sunny Italy', was the first of an astonishing list of over 1000 songs which flowed from him throughout a lifetime of over 100 years.

By 1909, he was working as a professional lyric writer for music publishers and soon he was writing melodies as well as words, though he could neither read nor write music (and never learned to do so). His piano playing was rudimentary and he only felt comfortable playing on the black keys. Eventually he acquired a piano with a built-in mechanical transposing device which, by a shifting lever, enabled him to 'play' in one key (usually F sharp) while the sound came out in another.

Irving Berlin's career and status moved into high gear in 1911 with a song called 'Alexander's Ragtime Band'. A massive hit, it marked Berlin as a major talent. Rumours grew that Puccini wanted to collaborate with him, and that George Bernard Shaw was interested in writing lyrics for him. Nothing came of either suggestion. Three years later he wrote his first Broadway show, *Watch Your Step*, and then built his own theatre. The Berlin legend was well on its way.

Irving Berlin could write for cinema audiences or live theatre. For Broadway he eventually wrote 17 musical shows, including the blockbusters *Annie Get Your Gun* and *Call Me Madam*, and provided some music for six others. His film scores were part of the very dawning of sound in the cinema. In 1927 Al Jolson sang Irving Berlin's '*Blue Skies*' in the first 'talkie', *The Jazz Singer*, and Berlin went on to provide music for 13 other movies. His film scores included three of the famous Fred Astaire and Ginger Rogers pairings.

In the late 1930s, Berlin was considering a musical with a storyline based around the four seasons. He conceived an idea for one winter song to be called 'White Christmas'. It was ready by 1940 and its first performance came on Christmas Day 1941 when Bing Crosby sang it on CBS radio. He recorded it in 1942 and in the same year sang it in the movie *Holiday Inn*, sitting at a piano in front of a fire. As he sang, there were intercut scenes of snow, a horse-drawn sleigh, children playing, Santa Claus and a beautifully decorated Christmas tree. Marjorie Reynolds sang with him (with a dubbed voice) and Crosby whistled an obbligato. The song went straight to the No. 1 position in radio charts and stayed there for 11 weeks. The following year it was awarded the Oscar for the best song of 1942. Bing Crosby's performance of 'White Christmas' was the best-selling single record in the world for over 50 years.

The effect of Crosby's mellow baritone, wistful but never mawkish, and the imagery of the song itself, enthused the public, who took to 'White Christmas' in a big way. It evoked instant nostalgia for how things once were, or might have been – for many of the people who listened to the song or sang it lovingly had no hope of ever seeing snow.

A hit song in 1941 became the focus of a full-scale movie in 1954. Bing Crosby, Rosemary Clooney, Vera-Ellen, Danny Kaye.

Although a white Christmas is comparatively rare, the association of snow and 25 December goes back to Charles Dickens' *Christmas Carol*, and even earlier to Clement Moore's poem, ''Twas the Night Before Christmas', written in 1822. For many, Berlin's song was a link to this fantasy world, and to the world depicted by American artist Norman Rockwell, where snowflakes fell gently through the beams of streetlights, horses breathed happy steam and children threw harmless snowballs. 'White Christmas' recalled fond memories, pleasant holiday times and family warmth.

Originally the song had a verse, in which the singer, on Christmas Eve, is among the orange and palm trees in the sun of Beverly Hills, but longs to be 'up North', for a real Christmas. The verse didn't make it onto the original Crosby recording and the song's appearance in *Holiday Inn* was picture-book midwinter, so the song's opening was gradually forgotten.

But there was more. As broadcast by Bing Crosby, the song was first heard just over two weeks after Pearl Harbor was bombed by the Japanese on 7 December 1941. The next day the United States declared war on Japan: America was at war. When troops serving overseas heard Berlin's song on the forces radio network as they spent Christmas 1942, their first overseas, far from their families and sweethearts, Bing Crosby, with the John Scott Trotter orchestra and the Darby singers, became the expression of their homesickness and longing for peace.

After the Second World War the popularity of 'White Christmas' remained undented. In 1945 and 1946 it was No. 1 in the charts. Paramount could see the potential for a whole movie to be called *White Christmas*. Bing Cosby and Fred Astaire had been co-stars in the earlier *Holiday Inn* movie, but Astaire was not available this time. Donald O'Connor agreed to replace him, but then became ill and had to withdraw. Danny Kaye stepped in and, along with Rosemary Clooney and Vera Ellen, made a colourful and lively quartet of stars.

Filmed in colour and wide-screen VistaVision, *White Christmas* came out in 1954. Some of the music was recycled Berlin, including of course 'White Christmas', but there were some new Berlin numbers too: 'The Best Things Happen While You're Dancing', 'Sisters', 'Snow', 'Love, You Didn't Do Right By Me' and 'Count Your Blessings Instead of Sheep'. Although lacking a spectacular storyline – four people staging a show to help an old buddy recoup business after a downturn – the movie was an attractive and pleasing piece of entertainment and became the highest grossing film of the year.

By family background, there was little connection between Irving Berlin and the religious significance of Christmas. Nor was this improved by the fact that his son, born in 1928, had died on Christmas Day aged only three weeks. His parents visited his grave every Christmas Day afterwards. Born Jewish, Irving Berlin escaped hypocrisy in creating America's two most popular Christian festival songs, 'Easter Parade' and 'White Christmas'. His integrity guided him to highlight the associated warmth of those times, rather than pretending to espouse the divinity they represented.

'White Christmas' has been performed in almost every conceivable music style: choral, orchestral, jazz (Charlie Parker), doo-wop (The Drifters) and reggae (Bob Marley). It has been sung by U2, Mandy Patinkin (in Yiddish), Otis Redding and even the Chipmunks. But Berlin, who didn't like rock'n'roll, wasn't pleased with Elvis Presley's 1957 version and wanted to advise people not to buy it.

Berlin had composed a song that became a radio broadcast, then a record, then a song within a film, then a song around which a film was built. Only one step remained, and it happened in 2002, when the Rodgers and Hammerstein Organisation, owners of Irving Berlin's music, selected 17 of his songs and commissioned writers to build them into a stage show based on the 1954 *White Christmas* film. Berlin's most famous song became a theatre musical.

It might be easier to name the people who *didn't* record 'White Christmas'. Some of those who *did* include Louis Armstrong, Chet Atkins, The Beach Boys, Tony Bennett, Michael Bolton, Garth Brooks, Michael Bublé, Charlotte Church, Rosemary Clooney, Perry Como, Doris Day, John Denver, Destiny's Child, Neil Diamond, Percy Faith, Ella Fitzgerald, The Four Tops, Connie Francis, Eydie Gormé, Lena Horne, Engelbert Humperdinck, Billy Idol, Chris Isaak, Burl Ives, Jack Jones, Elton John, Kiri Te Kanawa, Peggy Lee, Darlene Love, Henry Mancini, Barry Manilow, Mantovani, Bob Marley and the Wailers, Dean Martin, Johnny Mathis, Reba McEntire, Maureen McGovern, Bette Midler, the Glenn Miller Orchestra, the Mormon Tabernacle Choir, Anne Murray, Nina and Frederik, Charlie Parker, The Partridge Family, The Platters, Elvis Presley, Otis Redding, Jim Reeves, Kenny Rogers, Linda Ronstadt, Frank Sinatra, Kate Smith, Ringo Starr, Barbra Streisand, Sugababes, The Supremes, The Temptations, The Three Tenors, Caterina Valente, Frankie Valli and the Four Seasons, Andy Williams and Tammy Wynette.

Berlin died in 1989 aged 101. President Dwight D. Eisenhower had awarded him a gold medal, there had been six Academy Award nominations, one Tony and one Oscar. With no formal musical training, he had created a huge catalogue of songs, many of which had become a fixture in America's aural landscape. He had the ability to create hope, acknowledge regret, welcome humour and foster love and loyalty. In 1973, in a rare interview, Berlin told author Max Wilk that any new song had to be tried out on listeners and if they didn't like it, he'd change it, because 'I write to please the public'. With 'White Christmas', he certainly did just that.

Just some of Irving Berlin's songs

'Alexander's Ragtime Band', 'How Deep Is the Ocean', 'Blue Skies', 'White Christmas', 'Always', 'Anything You Can Do', 'There's No Business Like Show Business', 'Cheek to Cheek', 'Puttin' On the Ritz', 'A Pretty Girl is Like a Melody', 'Heat Wave', 'Easter Parade', 'Let's Face the Music and Dance', 'What'll I Do', 'Always', 'Remember' and 'God Bless America'.

Amazing Grace

How sweet the sound that sav'd a wretch like me!

JOHN NEWTON, TUNE ANON., 1779

A ship carrying slaves struck a storm so severe that the frightened captain called on God to help and in gratitude for his survival composed one of the world's favourite hymns. That is the legend – a potent mix of slavery, repentance and Christian authorship. It isn't entirely untruthful but upon examination, the story is a little longer than a one-sentence summary seems to indicate.

John Newton was born in London in 1725, the son of a commander on a merchant ship around the Mediterranean area. His mother died when he was seven, and he barely remembered the religious instruction she had tried to teach him in his early years. It was a sad and lonely childhood. At the age of 11, young John started going to sea with his father as a seaman apprentice. At 19 he was impressed (forced) into service on a warship. Newton hated this life, and after a short period deserted the ship but was captured and flogged. Young Newton then went to Sierra Leone and became a servant to a slave trader, which turned out to be an even worse life. Eventually a sea captain who had been a colleague of his father was able to extract him from the abusive employer.

But the connection with the slave trade remained. John Newton stayed at sea and, still in his twenties, became a captain of one of the ships carrying slaves to America. Up to 600 slaves at a time were transported in these vessels, often in appallingly inhuman conditions. Death from disease or suffocation was not uncommon, and fierce dogs often guarded the hatchways to attack any slaves who might incite their fellows to riot – if they were not shackled, as many were.

During one such voyage in 1748, the ship Newton was captaining encountered a severe storm. All livestock was lost overboard and the crew tied themselves to parts of the ship so that they weren't swept away as well. Newton experienced severe difficulty in steering, and as the storm increased and the fragility of the ship became more apparent, he began to be convinced that his vessel would sink and they would all die. Reaching back into half-forgotten lessons from his childhood about God's grace, a principle he had long relinquished, Newton cried out to the Almighty. His diary recorded that the words 'Lord have mercy upon us' were torn from him.

The ship survived, and John Newton with it. Reflecting on the incident later, he came to believe that, in his hour of need, God's grace had been directed towards him, and he had been saved from death by a greater power. His unhappy experiences had soured him against any belief in goodness or godliness but the storm, and the ship's seemingly miraculous survival, caused Newton to turn to Christianity. Curiously, his new attitude to life did not include any recognition that the enslavement of black people was wrong. Although now observing God's grace, he continued as a slave-trading captain for many more voyages.

In 1750 Newton married Mary Catlett and five years later gave up his seagoing life, though he remained close to the sea, becoming Surveyor of Tides at Liverpool, which involved Customs inspection and the apprehending of contraband. He embarked on a programme of self-education, learning, among other things, Latin, Greek and Hebrew. His 1748 near-death experience was not forgotten: each year he commemorated 10 May as the occasion of his acceptance of Christianity.

His interest in Christian matters broadened and deepened. He became friendly with a Calvinistic deacon and met the founder of Methodism, John Wesley. Newton began to consider a life of service in the church. Unable to gain admission to the Anglican clergy, he doggedly kept on trying until eventually he was accepted, ordained by the Bishop of Lincoln and took up an appointment as curate in Olney, Buckinghamshire.

The tune of 'John Brown's Body' has done service to at least two other songs. It was heard in 1855 as a hymn called 'Say Brothers Will You Meet Us on Canaan's Happy Shore'. Only a few years later, the tune became associated with poor John Brown, who had tried to abolish slavery by stealing weapons to give to black people to start their own revolt. He was hanged for treason in 1859. Then, when the American Civil War started in 1861, Julia Ward Howe set new words to the old tune and it became 'Mine Eyes Have Seen the Glory of the Coming of the Lord' – the Battle Hymn of the Republic.

Immediately successful in his new role, Newton drew weekly congregations which grew to such numbers that the church had to be enlarged.

Around 1767 John Newton became interested in writing hymns. The well-known poet William Cowper had come to live near him and the two men became friends. They began an amiable contest: each week one of them had to write the words for a new hymn. Legend persists that Newton's creation of 'Amazing Grace' was directly related to his memory of the frightening storm. Although this is possible, it can't really be proven since, over a period of 12 years, he composed over 200 other hymns, a volume of which was published in 1779, including 68 hymns of Cowper's, as the *Olney Hymns*. These were words only – Cowper and Newton were not musicians.

One original edition of the *Olney Hymns* survives in the University of Texas at Austin. It contains several hymns which became very popular, including 'How Sweet the Name of Jesus Sounds,' 'Glorious Things of Thee are Spoken' and another called 'Faith's Review and Expectation'. Its first three verses were:

> Amazing Grace! (how sweet the sound)
> That sav'd a wretch like me!
> I once was lost. But now am found
> Was blind, but now I see.
>
> 'Twas grace that taught my heart to fear,
> And grace my fears reliev'd;
> How precious did that grace appear,
> The hour I first believ'd.
>
> Thro' many dangers, toils and snares,
> I have already come;
> 'Tis grace has brought me safe thus far,
> And grace will lead me home.

It is believed that this hymn was sung at Newton's evening services but it is not clear which tune was employed. In the 50 years following, the hymn's title moved from the original 'Faith's Review and Expectation' to 'Amazing Grace' and it was published with the tune by which it is now known.

Applying newly written words to an extant tune was common practice in the days before global copyrights. Scholars have pored over exactly which tune John Newton's words were married to; one analyst even speculated that the melody could be related to a mournful slave song, sung during their nightmare journey in the ships. There is no provenance for this suggestion: the idea seemed to be driven by a wish to associate the hymn more closely with Newton's earlier career in slavery and his epiphany, disregarding the 30 years between.

It is generally believed that an old plantation melody called 'Loving Lambs', which was also known as 'New Britain', formed the basis of the tune that became what we now know as 'Amazing Grace'. That tune was itself believed to be of Scottish or Irish origin. Its pentatonic structure has strong affinity with bagpipes, and in its modern form it has indeed been played on this instrument and recorded with great success.

The text and its newly added tune were seen together in a 'shape-note' music book *Southern Harmony*, published in America in 1835. It was frequently sung during the American Civil War, and developed a significance for Cherokees, who in war conditions could not give their dead the full traditional rites, but developed the singing of 'Amazing Grace' as a partial replacement. Since then, the song has become familiar worldwide, with especial popularity in the United States. It is frequently used by human rights organisations, and its lines about being lost and found are considered very appropriate for Christian-managed substance abuse recovery programmes. The hymn holds a particular place in the esteem of African Americans, for whom slavery and the rise of the black population is central. The legend of 'Amazing Grace' is widely known and the hymn is fervently sung in black Christian congregations, who find in it the image of a white man brought to see the error of his ways regarding the enslavement of black people.

Newton's hymn had six verses. In modern times these have had a slight tidying up in punctuation, and in some versions a maverick seventh verse appears. This is from no less a source than Harriet Beecher Stowe. In her

As the *Titanic* sank in 1912, the ship's band played … what? Reports from survivors have never agreed. Was it 'Nearer My God to Thee', 'Abide with Me' or, as the last person believed to have left the ship alive avowed, 'Autumn'? Maritime analysts tend to dismiss the possibility of the band playing anything since the severely slanted surfaces of the sinking ship would have made it almost impossible for musicians to control their instruments.

1852 novel *Uncle Tom's Cabin* the character of Uncle Tom lifted a verse from another hymn, 'Jerusalem my Happy Home', and added it to 'Amazing Grace'. It worked so logically that many thought the verse was part of Newton's original.

> When we've been here ten thousand years,
> Bright shining as the sun,
> We've no less days to sing God's praise
> Than when we'd first begun.

In his later life, John Newton moved to London, where he preached to large congregations. By then he had undergone a change of heart about the morality of the slave trade and his ideals helped to influence William Wilberforce, who later became one of the leading abolitionists of slavery.

In an unsettling irony, the metaphor of Newton's line 'Was blind, but now I see' was reversed in real life: in later years he became physically blind. It didn't stop him preaching, however, and when he died in 1807, he was secure in his belief that, in death, the amazing grace of his God would indeed lead him 'home'.

Home Sweet Home

'Mid pleasures and palaces,
though we may roam.

HENRY ROWLEY BISHOP, 1823

Sir Henry Rowley Bishop didn't have great fortune in his own home life, with two failed marriages, but professionally, he was successful and famous. He composed over 100 operettas, ballets, symphonic works, and 17 operas, became an eminent professor and was the first composer to be knighted. But after all that, only one of his songs remains in people's memory.

Born in 1786, Bishop began training as a jockey but when still a teenager changed to studying music. By the age of 17 he had composed an opera, *Angelina*, and then worked as a musician in most of the prestigious theatres in London. In 1810 he became musical director of Covent Garden Theatre, later known as the Royal Opera House. In 1821 he was commissioned to edit a volume of 'national melodies', eventually entitled *Melodies of Various Nations*. Towards the end of the project he realised that the collection contained tunes from all over Europe but none from Sicily. So quietly, without saying a word, he composed a melody that he judged would sound 'Sicilian' and put it into the album. Thus began the chequered history of 'Home Sweet Home'.

When he got round to composing his opera *Clari*, Bishop resurrected the 'Sicilian' melody and gave it a prominent role. *Clari* was performed at Covent Garden Theatre in 1823, and his earlier deception came back to bite him. The story of *Clari* was that of a naive village maiden enticed to a castle by a nobleman who had promised marriage. At the castle she was given gifts aplenty, but no wedding ring. Sadly, and with the beginnings of disillusion, the maiden sang of the sweetness and security she once knew. On opening night, 8 May 1823, singer Ann Marie Tree as Clari gave the first performance of 'Home Sweet Home'.

The melody was first heard in the overture, then Clari sang it, and then the melody appeared again three more times during the course of the opera. This repetition of a melody or portions of it throughout a longer work was an unusual composing technique at the time. Because of it, Bishop has been seen by some as the originator of the 'theme song', and also possibly as a pioneer of 'song plugging'.

As an opera, *Clari* was not notably successful – except for that one song. The public loved 'Home Sweet Home'. Over 100,000 copies of the sheet music were sold in the first year after the opera was premiered. But because some smart research had revealed that the melody had previously been published as a tune from Sicily, there was a belief that the tune was traditional and therefore non-copyright and pirated editions began to appear.

John Howard Payne, who wrote the immortal words for 'Home Sweet Home'.

Henry Bishop's publishers went to court to obtain an injunction against the illegal editions, and Bishop gave the court sworn testimony of the truth: that the melody was actually his own composition. He was believed, and the tune was legally declared to be the composition of Henry Rowley Bishop.

Bishop's collaborator, who provided the lyrics for *Clari*, was an American called John Howard Payne. Born in 1791, he wanted to be an actor, a career with which his parents were not comfortable. While still at university he started writing poems and publishing essays. Bankruptcy in the family cut short his education and Payne took the opportunity to take his first acting job. Although this debut was a great success, it was followed by a long and dispiriting period of unemployment.

At the age of 23, Payne borrowed money and sailed to England, intending to stay a year. One year became 20, during which he abandoned acting and instead became a full-time writer, creating, adapting or translating over 60 theatre works. John Howard Payne and Henry Bishop were acquainted, and although London-based, Payne also spent time in Paris, sharing an apartment for a time with American writer Washington Irving. In Paris, Bishop and Payne had once attended a ballet called *Clari – or the Promise of Marriage*. It was this that formed the basis for Bishop's subsequent opera, with a libretto by Payne.

Although Payne's level of work seemed considerable, his finances were not. After scant payment for his contribution to *Clari* and because, in the fashion of the time, his name was not listed as lyricist on the sheet music of 'Home Sweet Home', he became disillusioned and, borrowing money again for his passage, he returned to America. There he eked out a life of sufficient respectability for some years until eventually he was appointed American consul to Tunis in Africa in 1842, a post he held for 10 years before he died.

In spite of the court case, there were still some conflicts about 'Home Sweet Home'. In *Melodies of Various Nations* the tune appeared as 'a Sicilian air with words by Thomas H. Bayley, "To the home of my childhood in sorrow I came".' Two years later, a published version of 'Home Sweet Home' has the line 'Adapted from a national melody and arranged by Henry R. Bishop'. But the general feeling is that these references were Bishop's deliberate fudging of his later admitted deception.

'Home Sweet Home' gradually became immensely popular, and not just in England. American soldiers in the Civil War took a particular liking to it, as have later soldiers of other nations in almost every war since. Famous operatic divas of the time, such as Adelina Patti and Jenny Lind, included it

> 'Show Me the Way to Go Home', composed in London in 1925, has a range of only four notes.

in their concerts all over the world, as did divas of later eras – Nellie Melba, Joan Sutherland, Kiri Te Kanawa. People far from familiar surroundings found warmth and solace in the simple and direct message. And although there was no paucity of sentimental songs in the late 19th century, it is possible that the stream of other songs about home may have been related to the impact made by 'Home Sweet Home'.

Henry Rowley Bishop went on to great things. In 1841 he was appointed Professor of Music at Edinburgh University, and a year later Queen Victoria dubbed him Sir Henry. He reached the top rung in 1848, when he moved from Edinburgh to become Professor of Music at Oxford University, where he remained until his death in 1855.

The manuscript score of *Clari* used in Bishop's court case is held in the Sibley Library at the Eastman School of Music at the University of Rochester, New York. In 1923, a celebration was held there to mark the centenary of *Clari* – and 'Home Sweet Home'. Items of Bishop's works were played, with audiovisuals, and the manuscript itself was highlighted in a glass case. The locals of East Hampton, New York believe that during his childhood John Howard Payne spent time in a picturesque house said to have belonged to his grandfather. The house still stands, preserved as a memorial to Payne, and known as the Home Sweet Home Museum.

'Mid pleasures and palaces though we may roam,
Be it ever so humble, there's no place like home;
A charm from the sky seems to hallow us there,
Which, seek through the world, is ne'er met with elsewhere.
Home, home, sweet, sweet home!
There's no place like home, oh, there's no place like home!

An exile from home, splendor dazzles in vain;
Oh, give me my lowly thatched cottage again!
The birds singing gaily, that came at my call
Give me them and the peace of mind, dearer than all!
Home, home, sweet, sweet home!
There's no place like home, oh, there's no place like home!

I gaze on the moon as I tread the drear wild,
And feel that my mother now thinks of her child,
As she looks on that moon from our own cottage door
Through the woodbine, whose fragrance shall cheer me no more.
Home, home, sweet, sweet home!
There's no place like home, oh, there's no place like home!

How sweet 'tis to sit 'neath a fond father's smile,
And the caress of a mother to soothe and beguile!
Let others delight 'mid new pleasure to roam,
But give me, oh, give me, the pleasures of home,
Home, home, sweet, sweet home!
There's no place like home, oh, there's no place like home!

To thee I'll return, overburdened with care;
The heart's dearest solace will smile on me there;
No more from that cottage again will I roam;
Be it ever so humble, there's no place like home.
Home, home, sweet, sweet home
There's no place like home, oh, there's no place like home!

Moon River

Wider than a mile,
I'm crossing you in style some day.

HENRY MANCINI, JOHNNY MERCER, 1961

Was there ever a real Holly Golightly? Apparently, yes. During the 1940s, American Dorian Leigh was described as the most famous model in the world. Writers on beauty ranked the order as Vivien Leigh, Hedy Lamarr and then Dorian Leigh.

Dorian Leigh Parker was the daughter of a chemical engineer who raised his four daughters as strict Baptists – no smoking, drinking, swearing or make-up. But their mother, Elizabeth, was tall and attractive, and the Parker girls slowly grew into striking beauties. Dorian, the eldest daughter, had an early marriage to a college sweetheart, two children, then divorced and worked as a copywriter for a film company. But she was pretty, and when she got to hear what models were being paid, she approached an agency.

Now known as Dorian Leigh, at 27 she was well past the usual age for youthful beauty, and she was short, even petite, when models were (and still are) traditionally taller than most men. But she had a face that was classically boned, eyes of hypnotic blue, intriguing eyebrows and an air of feminine mystery. She became a sensation as a model, reaching the cover of *Harper's Bazaar* in 1944, and reigning for the rest of that decade and the next.

Photographers discovered her amazing chameleon qualities: she could become anything required by the context of the photo shoot. As Sir Cecil Beaton wrote in his book *Photobiography*, she 'conveys a remarkable variety of moods … the sweetness of an eighteenth century pastel, the allure of a Sargent portrait, or the poignancy of some unfortunate woman who sat for Modigliani'. She was courted by Revlon cosmetics and became 'the Revlon woman' and star of the company's internationally sensational 'Fire and Ice' campaign.

Having long discarded the restrictions of her Baptist upbringing, Dorian Leigh oscillated between New York and Paris and every other headquarters of high fashion, rapidly gaining a reputation for being socially dynamic – what in modern times might be called a party girl. Socially she moved at the top international level, with Charlie Chaplin, Coco Chanel, Harry Belafonte, Dizzy Gillespie, Diana Vreeland, Irving Shaw, Robert Graves, Howard Hughes, Buddy Rich and Truman Capote, then the hottest young writer in New York. And there were the men. During her long life of more than eight decades, Dorian Leigh had several husbands (with one of whom she became a titled marquise) and a reputed legion of A-list affairs. She was said to have a generous disposition, and her favourite indoor game wasn't chess. Dorian Leigh was the world's first supermodel, before the word itself was even invented. When her own modelling days began to fade, she established an agency, and discovered, among others, Twiggy and Verushka.

When based in New York, Dorian Leigh lived a somewhat frenetic lifestyle in Lexington Avenue and relied on the co-operation of a friendly little shop nearby to take her phone messages. Truman Capote was fascinated with her, and was a frequent visitor. He learned to gain entry to her apartment through the fire escape, and she would come home and find him playing with her cats. Reflecting that her life was what Oscar Wilde's Lady Bracknell would have described as 'crowded with incident', Capote coined his nickname for her, 'Happy-go-lucky'. And inside his head a character began to form – a woman with a more than liberal take on the usual rules of life, behaviour, morality and work. His familiarity with the zany glamour of Dorian Leigh, and the echo of his nickname for her, helped to create one of the memorable characters of 20th-century fiction, Holly Golightly.

She was introduced to readers when Capote's *Breakfast at Tiffany's* was published in 1958. It was a remarkable piece of work, risqué for the 1950s. Word spread very quickly that Holly was directly based on Dorian Leigh. Holly has no compunction about mentioning her adventures in bed, she accepts that black men can be attractive, she lacks any guilt about stealing a friend's man and has no inhibitions about gays and lesbians. Her final bittersweet disappearance is followed by the later discovery of a decorative carving from deep in a jungle, a carving that unmistakably resembles Holly Golightly. *Time* described her as somewhere between Lolita and Auntie Mame.

After the book was published, work began very soon on the movie, which was released three years later in 1961. Capote wanted Marilyn Monroe to play Holly Golightly. By then his friendship with Monroe had acquainted him with her quality of vulnerability, also perceptible in the character of Holly Golightly (though not, apparently, in the real Dorian Leigh). But Capote did not have the authority to insist and was overruled by executives at Paramount, who contracted Audrey Hepburn. Initially dissatisfied with the leading lady, Capote was even more horrified at changes made in his story – the whitewashing of Holly's moral freedoms, and particularly the ending, where Holly was persuaded to remain in New York.

Audrey Hepburn, as Holly Golightly, sings 'Moon River' in Breakfast at Tiffany's, *1961.*

The choice of Hepburn made a slightly uncanny link with the inspiration for Holly. Dorian Leigh's sister Suzy, 17 years younger, had grown from a gawky and sickly asthmatic into a tall and breathtaking copper-haired beauty. Without a shred of jealousy, Dorian Leigh energetically promoted her baby sister in the modelling world, with the result that Suzy Parker also became an international top model. Her legendary status, growing from an ugly duckling beginning to spectacular success, and her relationship with top photographer Richard Avedon, became the inspiration for the 1956 movie, *Funny Face*, in which Audrey Hepburn plays virtually the real life of Suzy Parker.

Whatever Capote's disappointments, nobody had any complaint about the choice of the movie's composer and lyricist. Henry Mancini and Johnny Mercer had impeccable track records. Mancini was responsible for such hits as the 'Pink Panther' theme, the 'Baby Elephant Walk', the 'Hatari' music, the 'Peter Gunn' theme and 'Days of Wine and Roses', to name but a few. Johnny Mercer had provided the words for 'Cool Cool Cool of the Evening', 'Hooray for Hollywood', 'One for My Baby', 'Autumn Leaves', 'That Old Black Magic' and a dozen others. Mancini and Mercer eventually were awarded four Oscars each. One, in 1962, for best movie song, was for 'Moon River', from the 1961 movie, *Breakfast at Tiffany's*.

Audrey Hepburn's singing voice was threadlike, and extremely limited in range, though always in tune. Like Marilyn Monroe, Audrey had also once sung 'Happy Birthday' to President John F. Kennedy. But Johnny Mercer faced some obstacles in getting to a final concept of a song for her. He had grown up in Savannah and, with memories of its waterways, started a song called 'Blue River', then discovered that the title was already in use elsewhere. He tried using the opening words 'I'm Holly' but discarded that as banal. Mancini took a month to compose exactly the right melody to suit the waif-like good-time girl character. In the movie, Hepburn sang the song herself, sitting with a guitar on the fire escape of a New York apartment, and the result, besides being Oscar-winning, was absolutely charming.

In the movie *Singin' in the Rain* actress Jean Hagen played Lina Lamont, an early film star, who, when sound came to movies, was revealed to have a voice so brutal that a younger woman, played by Debbie Reynolds, was hired to dub her songs. But Reynolds' own singing voice was not considered to be rich enough, and singer Betty Noyes was brought in to dub for Reynolds who was supposedly dubbing for Lamont.

Mancini later reported that after the very first preview screening of *Breakfast at Tiffany's* the president of Paramount Pictures puffed a cigar and announced that the song had to be removed. The normally gentle Audrey Hepburn told him firmly that it would be over her dead body. In spite of the movie's extraordinary success, Paramount seemed to be still a bit cagey about Audrey's singing and on the released 'soundtrack' album, her simple vocal-plus-guitar was replaced by a sweeping Mancini orchestral version.

But with or without Hepburn, the song itself soared in popularity. In the first flush of its release, over one million copies of the sheet music were sold. Andy Williams' recording and subsequent performances became one of his biggest hits and the song title became the name of his own theatre in Missouri, which also features a Moon River Grill. Five hundred other known recorded versions exist, including those of Frank Sinatra, Louis Armstrong, Judy Garland, Sarah Vaughan and Sarah Brightman. After Audrey Hepburn died in 1993, her own original track was released for the first time. And a large river inlet in Savannah, near where lyricist Johnny Mercer lived, was renamed Moon River in his honour.

'Moon River' crops up in unexpected places. Movies made in places like Japan, Spain and Korea have featured it. It has been heard in the television series *Sex and the City* and *The Simpsons*. In the 1985 movie *Fletch*, Chevy Chase croons the tune while having his rectum examined, and comedienne Joan Rivers has presented her own self-deprecating humorous version: 'Joan Rivers, older than the sky ...'

People have sometimes asked about the meaning of the phrase 'huckleberry friend'. As a child, Johnny Mercer picked huckleberries (like wild blueberries) in the summer. To him, the berries had a personal connection with a carefree boyhood, strengthened by association with Mark Twain's character Huckleberry Finn, who lived a carefree life along the banks of the Mississippi River. The implication was that Holly Golightly, who was actually of hillbilly stock, and Huckleberry Finn might well have been friends, if ever they had met.

Twinkle, Twinkle, Little Star

How I wonder what you are.
Up above the world so high.

ANN AND JANE TAYLOR, 1838

Ann and Jane Taylor lived in Suffolk in the late 18th and early 19th centuries. Like a somewhat reduced version of the Brontë sisters, both young women were homebodies, dedicated to writing – mostly poems and hymns for children. Besides their natural inclination towards authorship, they had to write down everything concerned with day-to-day living because of their mother's deafness.

The sisters' published books, among them *Original Poems for Infant Minds*, *Rhymes for the Nursery* and *Hymns for Infant Minds*, were popular and successful in the early 1800s. But, unlike the Brontës, only one piece of their work ever achieved worldwide fame.

The two women normally wrote jointly so neither was identified as the author of a simple five-verse poem called 'The Star', which appeared in the 1806 publication *Rhymes for the Nursery*. Authorship has usually been ascribed to 'the Taylor sisters', though Ann Taylor's son Josiah Gilbert was later confident that his aunt, Jane, was the main author. Either way, *Rhymes for the Nursery* was sufficiently successful to go into 27 editions.

Over 30 years after it was first published, 'The Star' was set to music. By a strange coincidence (we cannot know if it was deliberate) the Taylors' verse rhythm fitted perfectly with an old French folk tune that had been published in 1761 as an instrumental piece, and was later published with the words 'Ah vous dirai-je Maman' in 1774. Over 60 years after that, in 1838, a book called *The Singing Master: First Class Tune Book* was published, with the words of 'Twinkle, Twinkle, Little Star' now set to be sung to the old French tune. A popular misconception existed that the tune was composed by Mozart, but this turned out not to be true. Mozart did later write a set of variations on the same old French tune.

THE STAR
(original text, 1806)

Twinkle, twinkle, little star,
How I wonder what you are!
Up above the world so high,
Like a diamond in the sky.

When the blazing sun is gone,
When he nothing shines upon,
Then you show your little light,
Twinkle, twinkle, all the night.

Then the traveller in the dark,
Thanks you for your tiny spark,
He could not see which way to go,
If you did not twinkle so.

In the dark blue sky you keep,
And often through my curtains peep,
For you never shut your eye,
Till the sun is in the sky.

As your bright and tiny spark,
Lights the traveller in the dark,
Though I know not what you are,
Twinkle, twinkle, little star.

Since then, millions throughout the world have come to know the simple tune, if not always with the Taylors' words. Before 'The Star' made its change from poem to song, a centuries-old poem about a black sheep came into print in 1744 and moved closer to immortality by being hooked onto the same French tune as 'Twinkle, Twinkle', to be followed in 1834 by a clever little 'Alphabet Song', showing that all 26 letters, like the sheep and the twinkling star, could be fitted to 'Ah vous dirai-je Maman'.

Perhaps the structure of the old French tune invites various words: there have certainly been numerous parodies of 'Twinkle, Twinkle'. A version in Latin had a brief vogue ('Mica mica parva stella') and Lewis Carroll's Mad Hatter sang his version, about a twinkling little bat, who resembles a teatray in the sky. The Muppets also took a swipe, but one of the more charming variations is that familiar to children in the northern parts of Canada, who sing :

Twinkle, twinkle, Northern Lights,
Shimmer in the arctic nights,
Up above the clouds so high
Green blue ribbons in the sky.

And perhaps the variation to silence them all, John Raymond Carson's satirical version in Orotund-speak:

Scintillate, scintillate, globule vivific,
Fain would I fathom thy nature specific,
Loftily poised in the ether capacious
Strongly resembling a gem carbonaceous.
(Copyright 2002 George Carson & Ann Hough Family Organization)

Begin The Beguine

*It brings back the sound
of music so tender.*

Cole Porter, 1935

In both words and lyrics, Cole Porter was one of the supreme masters of song-writing. By 1935, he was well established as a leading contributor to the popular American song genre. He already had an impressive collection of hits – 'I Get a Kick out of You', 'Miss Otis Regrets', 'Night and Day', 'Love for Sale', 'Anything Goes', 'You're the Top' – and he still had 20 years of composing left.

When he was creating a new song, Porter's fine sense of lyric and vivid imagination often drew some impetus from his exotic travels. 'What is This Thing Called Love?' was suggested by a native dance in Morocco's Marrakesh, 'The Kling-Kling Bird on the Divi-Divi Tree' was seen and heard in Jamaica, and music for his *Judgment of Paris* ballet arose from native rhythms heard on the island of Bali. When he was committed to writing a new show called *Jubilee* to open on Broadway in 1935, he needed time to concentrate away from distractions. Never one to eschew comfort, and wealthy enough to afford it, Porter and his wife Linda booked a four-month Pacific cruise on the *Franconia*. They required a cabin with a piano in it, and they also took writer Moss Hart with them.

In between working on the new show, Porter did allow for a few distractions. During the trip he soaked in hot mineral pools in New Zealand, met feathered chieftains in Papua New Guinea, had a smallpox scare in Singapore, was rickshawed by extravagantly dressed and painted Africans in Durban, and gazed in wonder at posters in Madagascar claiming a cure for syphilis. But there was also work. Moss Hart later reported, 'I learned to my chagrin that the jaunty and debonair world of

Cole Porter disappeared completely when he was at work and that Linda Porter was as stern and jealous a guardian of that work as Cole Porter himself.'

One part of their journey took them to Indonesia, specifically the settlement of Kalabahai on the Indonesian islands of Alor, north of Australia. The ship's passengers met the locals and were treated to a performance. The natives of the area had splendid costumes and a repertoire of intricate dances, performed with polish. One of these, a dance of war, impressed Cole Porter and its sounds and its image remained with him as the ship sailed away. Simultaneously, there came from the back of his mind a memory of a nightclub performance he had seen in Paris – black dancers from Martinique performing a type of slow rumba known as a beguine. The word, related to French, originally meant covered or hooded but had come to imply flirtation.

On the Indonesian island of Alor, the natives of Kalabahai inspired Cole Porter (centre) with the rhythm which became 'Begin the Beguine' in 1935.

Quite quickly, Porter seamlessly melded the two elements into a complete song, which he called 'Begin the Beguine'. Its debut performance was in the cabin of a liner, somewhere between Indonesia and Fiji. At 108 bars, it was an extraordinarily long song. Moss Hart, hearing it in the cabin for the first time, later said he had thought it had ended when it was only halfway through.

The musical *Jubilee* was inspired by the recent celebrations in Britain commemorating the 25th anniversary of the coronation of King George V and Queen Mary. The show told of a fictional kingdom celebrating such an anniversary but the royal family, tired of formalities, disguised themselves as 'ordinary people' and went walkabout to experience real life.

Jubilee opened in October 1935, but was not one of Porter's great successes. This is generally thought to be because the leading lady, Mary Boland, left the company to pursue a film career, and no appropriate 'draw' could be found to replace her. However, two of the show's songs have survived, and become Cole Porter classics: 'Just One of Those Things' and 'Begin the Beguine'.

'Begin the Beguine' was staged as a lavish production number, in a 'Café Martinique' night club. June Knight sang it, not in native costume, but a stylish 1930s petal-layered dress of pale fabric, trimmed with sequins in diagonal rows, halter topped with an extravagantly ribbonned and feathered strap. *The Times* mentioned the melody's 'hints of distant splendours', but 'Begin the Beguine' might have faded from view with the show. Three years later, however, it made a very big impact indeed, courtesy of band leader Artie Shaw.

Shaw was then only 28, and a long way from being the jazz legend he later became. But part of that legend began with Shaw's recording of 'Begin the Beguine'. Although *Jubilee* closed early, after 169 performances, sufficient people remembered 'Begin the Beguine' to be asking Artie Shaw if his band could play it. Eventually, Shaw had an arranger create music charts for his band to play the tune, but he decided to give the beguine rhythm more of a swing feel. The first night the band played it in a ballroom, they knew from the buzz that this number was going to work.

But recording it wasn't so easy. The recording company Shaw was contracted to was not impressed with 'Begin the Beguine', considered it of little value and grudgingly allowed it only as the B side to Shaw's recording of 'The Indian Love Call'. But within a very short time, word reached the company that record buyers greatly preferred the B side of the disc. The 'Beguine', so reluctantly recorded, quickly went into hundreds of juke boxes and sold millions of records. It was a tremendous hit and topped the American charts for six weeks.

Shaw's recording was certainly what made the song world famous, as well as launching his own fame. He soon reached the status of Benny Goodman, who also recorded the tune, as did the bands of Harry James, Tommy Dorsey, Xavier Coat, Paul Whiteman and Glenn Miller. In later years, Shaw reportedly felt he'd become saddled with the tune, since audiences still wanted it every night, but it helped to make him wealthy, and certainly didn't do Cole Porter any harm either.

During the 12th century, some women in the Netherlands formed themselves into a worshipful group called the Beguines. Not formally acknowledged as nuns, they led lives of devotion, celibacy and charitable work, but were not permanently bound to their calling and could leave the group whenever they wished. More communities of Beguines developed throughout the following centuries, and although their numbers have dwindled in recent times, some communities still exist. The 800 years since their beginnings have clouded the original reason for their name, and several conflicting explanations exist. It could be coincidence that the Beguines have the same name as an evocative Martinique rhythm. But whatever the reason for their name, the Beguines have shown no affinity for Cole Porter songs or dancing the rumba.

It's impossible to say what makes a song successful. The public, and the rest of the music industry, certainly didn't agree with Artie Shaw's recording company. Neither did the movie moguls at MGM, whose 1940 *Broadway Melody* featured Fred Astaire and Eleanor Powell in a spectacular dance sequence to Porter's song. The famous Andrews Sisters gave it a bounce for its money, and Ella Fitzgerald's and Frank Sinatra's versions are considered to be classic renditions of the song's sophistication – and supreme examples of the singers' own talents. In 1981 the Spanish singing star Julio Iglesias, who has sold over 250 million records, recorded a lush and sultry version of 'Begin the Beguine' which was a major hit in Europe.

The song somehow suggests sexual dalliance, or seduction, while also being an aural invitation to take to the dance floor – in the 1930s and 1940s when foxtrots were still trotting. Musical analysts, having got over the sheer length of 'Begin the Beguine', were dismayed that its structure was not in the traditional section plan of A, A, B, A, but a more sophisticated A, A, B, A1, C, C1, B, A. Yet there was nothing but praise for the song when Porter died in 1964. *Time* said that 'Begin the Beguine' was 'structured as artfully as a classical sonata, the theme elaborated and subtly expanded each time it returns, developed until it finally crests and crashes in soul-satisfying splendor'.

In her book *Travels with Cole Porter*, Jean Howard reported that when Cole arrived in Spain in 1956, the Customs officer who inspected his passport, shrieked, 'Cole Porter! "Begin the Beguine"!', then kissed his fingers and began to sing the song.

Besides the royalties, that was all any composer could wish for.

God Save the King/Queen

Happy and glorious,
Long to reign over us.

ANON.

'God Save the King' is sung to a centuries-old melody, referred to in the *Oxford Companion to Music* as 'the best-known tune in the world'. The melody's ancestor can be detected in an ancient free-rhythm plainsong whose words allude to the coronation of Solomon, and which also survives in a well-known anthem in the canton of Geneva.

Before the song settled into England, similar versions of the tune already existed across Europe along with words in French or German referring to appropriate rulers, for example 'Heil dir im Siegerkranz' in Prussia and 'Grand Dieu, sauve le roi' sung at Versailles for Louis XIV in 1686. Two years later a recognisably similar version of the tune was performed for King James II in Britain, and considering the family connections, it is possible that early elements of the French version drifted in from Versailles. James II's mother, Henrietta Maria, was the sister of Louis XIII, so James and Louis were cousins.

But the usual beginning point for the recognisable tune, with the words to which Britain is accustomed, was first seen in print in 1744 in the *Thesaurus Musicus*. The first known public performance was at Drury Lane theatre in September 1745, three years after the first performance of Handel's *Messiah* and six months after the debut of 'Rule Britannia'.

No one composer has ever been known, so the tune cannot be copyrighted. Hence, the melody we know as 'God Save the King/Queen' has been used for various purposes by 20 other non-British nations and by various composers.

The British title, 'God Save the King', is a slight variation from the Hebrew (from the books of Samuel and Kings), which became a familiar phrase in English after Tyndale's translations of the Old Testament was printed in the 1530s and then after the King James Bible appeared in 1611. The phrase later became a maritime 'challenge and reply' password, answered by the phrase, 'Long to reign over us'.

Like the tune, the words have no specific identifiable author. It is generally accepted that the currently recognised tune and words are the result of many fragments already in popular knowledge, which over a long period of time dovetailed into a smooth entity. After coming out in print in 1745, 'God Save the King' was rapidly accepted in England. Various factions created different sets of words, but the general aim of esteeming the monarch and wishing him/her well became established. Quite soon it was commonplace that the 'anthem' be played or sung on formal, ritual and royal social occasions, including going to the theatre.

The reign of King George III (1760–1820) included the well-publicised periods of his mental illness, which resulted in enormously enhanced use of and enthusiasm for the 'anthem'. The combination of his popularity and vulnerability did a great deal to spread knowledge of the song, because King George's problems were known to his subjects and caused great concern. During his bad times, fervent singing of 'God Save the King' was intended to do exactly that. When he recovered his mental health, the song was sung and played joyfully everywhere the king went – in the streets, in the churches, even by a band on a boat when he went for a swim.

The much-loved King George III of England, for whom 'God Save The King' became an anthem.

The sheer frequency of the song's performance gradually made it an indispensable ingredient of ceremonial events of all kinds, although no law or proclamation decreed that 'God Save the King' had become official. This was partly because the concept of a national anthem didn't really exist then. For centuries, nations had flags and songs of loyalty, but the idea of a national anthem, which could be described as the musical equivalent of a flag, was virtually unknown until Britain developed one.

The drift of 'God Save the King' into being Britain's official anthem was hardly discernible and no definite date can be cited. In 2003 the Lord Chamberlain's office in Britain, admitted that 'some of the detail has been lost over time'. But 1825 has been mentioned as the year that the song was first described as the national anthem, and it made its first appearance at a British coronation in 1831 when William IV was crowned.

Once it was established as a national anthem, the popularity of 'God Save the King/Queen' in Britain was enormous. One notably massive performance took place in the Halifax Cloth Hall in 1856. An assembly of 330 singers, and an orchestra of 500, were joined by a 24,700-strong chorus and an audience of 8000 – a total of 33,530 performers. The sound was described as 'majestic'. Another extravagant outing in 1843 featured the anthem played by the band of the Horse Guards. Their instruments included large kettle drums made of silver, at the time valued at £525 each, which has been calculated to be the equivalent of $NZ85,000.

In Britain there have been many variations in the song, mainly new versions of words: 150 of these exist. The fervent loyalty Queen Victoria inspired resulted in 18 different versions of the anthem during her reign, commemorating various events in her life: engagement, marriage, birth of children, widowhood, jubilees. Sample opening lines include:

In general, attempts in Britain to 'modernise' the traditional words have met with complete disdain from the public. In 1931 the Chancellor of the Exchequer made clear that the Establishment would take no part in any arguments about lyrics: 'the words to which the tune is sung are *no* part of the National Anthem. It is only the *tune itself* which is the National Anthem.'

On Britain's royal maid,
Love's brightest smile displayed …

Lord, Thy best blessings shed,
On our Queen's youthful head …

God Save our Gracious Queen,
Blessed with a brow serene ...

Oh Lord Thy blessings shed,
On royal Albert's head ...

Oh, Lord! Her consort bless,
Grant him in happiness ...

Our royal widow bless,
God guard the fatherless ...

Sorrow and joy her lot,
Yet Thee she ne-er forgot,
Wife Mother Queen ...

These and the other 11 versions that eulogised Victoria were so specific that they did not survive past her reign. Neither did the 'novelty bustle' she was given, with a built-in music box which played 'God Save the Queen' from under her gown.

Not able to be copyrighted in England, the melody of 'God Save the King' had gained attention in America, whence it had travelled before the Declaration of Independence. It was first printed in America in 1761, long after it had been first seen in England. As in England, many differing sets of words – at least 20 versions – became attached to the tune, with such titles as 'God save America', 'God save George Washington', 'Hail God-like Washington', 'God save the Thirteen States', 'God save the President', 'Hail thou auspicious day' and 'Fame Let thy Trumpet Sound'. But all these were overshadowed as a result of an incident in 1831.

American music publisher Lowell Mason asked a theological student, Samuel Smith, to write a new song for a children's choir at the Park Street Church in Boston. Mason gave Smith some hymn books whose tunes

Nearly a century after Britain, America gained a national anthem in 1931. 'The Star-spangled Banner' and 'God Save the King/Queen' share one peculiarity: neither mentions the name of the country whose anthem it is. And the British anthem is a waltz, although 3/4 time is not usually considered to be an adrenalin-stirrer.

he might use as inspiration. In one of those books, Samuel Smith saw a song with German words 'Heil, Dir im Siegerkranz' and took a liking to its simple straightforward tune. Aware that it was a patriotic song, Smith was fired to write verses of a similar patriotic nature, but about America.

Half an hour later, he had completed a set of words that perfectly fitted the tune in the book in front of him. He called it 'America'. The song was printed in 1832 as part of the publication called *The Choir, or Union Collection of Church Music*. The title 'America' fairly quickly became replaced by the song's first line: 'My country 'tis of thee'. After its debut by the children's choir for whom it was intended, the song spread. Schools sang it, and it was heard at patriotic meetings, social gatherings, even funerals, and eventually in military camps and during battle. America had a new hit, a patriotic song that achieved a popularity second only to 'The Star-spangled Banner'.

Some time after the song had settled into public awareness, Samuel Smith was occasionally identified as pro-British because he had used a tune with a strong affinity to Britain. Smith's surprised response was that he had seen the melody originally with German words and had no idea of its significance to the British. This is quite easy to believe since the melody had been used in Prussia and 'God Save the King' had been identified as an unofficial British anthem only five years before Lowell Mason gave the book of hymn tunes to Smith. Given the slowness of international communication at the time, Smith could hardly have known that the song had become 'official' in an English coronation that same year. Harvard University holds the original manuscript of 'My Country 'Tis of Thee', which is classified as an honoured document.

Samuel Smith was not the only person to use the ancient tune and bring it to musical heights. The melody has been 'borrowed' by numerous composers, and can be heard in some works of Beethoven, Debussy, Haydn, Brahms, Thalberg, Paganini, Weber, Verdi and Donizetti. The same tune is also the national anthem of Liechtenstein. So far this has not caused any confusion at Olympic Games.

God Save our gracious King/Queen,
Long live our noble King/Queen,
God save the King.
Send him victorious
Happy and Glorious
Long to reign over us
God save the King.

My country 'tis of thee
Sweet land of liberty,
Of thee I sing.
Land where my fathers died
Land of the pilgrims' pride
From every mountainside
Let freedom ring!

I Don't Know How To Love Him

What to do, how to move him.

ANDREW LLOYD WEBBER, TIM RICE, 1970

Mary Magdalene is a very shadowy figure, historically speaking. The first words, a very few of them, written about her appeared 100 years after her death. That hasn't, however, stopped people deciding things about her. Speculation, interpretation, myth and legend have gathered around her.

Was Mary of Magdala a woman of easy virtue? Did she marry Jesus and bear children, as suggested in the book *The Holy Blood and the Holy Grail?* Was she, and not a goblet, actually the Holy Grail? Nobody knows. One of the stories held that, regretting the behaviour of her earlier years, and reflecting on the sadness of her life, she repented. This caused her to weep, so painters often depicted her as a tearful woman. In 1969 she was canonised as the saint of repentant sinners and a year later, she, or rather her image, became the progenitor of a hit song.

Her name has several variations. The *Catholic Encyclopaedia* prefers Magdalene and the Cambridge University college named for her retains this spelling, though the similarly named Oxford University college shortens the name to Magdalen. In some places the 'g' was dropped in pronunciation so the name became 'maudlin'. The Oxford college uses this version. In English this word came to describe someone unnecessarily sad. Maudlin still means that; when used in that context, the spellings have followed the pronunciation. In earlier centuries, women who had fallen from grace became known as 'mawdelens' and the word surfaced as the name for some institutions which looked after 'fallen women'.

Among the hundreds of writers and painters intrigued by the Mary Magdalen legend were British musician Andrew Lloyd Webber and lyricist Tim Rice. Lloyd Webber was always comfortable with Christian-orientated music. His father was a Professor and Examiner in Theory and Composition at the Royal College of Music, his mother was a piano teacher and both Andrew and his cellist brother Julian were very familiar with Church of England hymns, psalms, oratorio and ritual. Tim Rice came from a slightly different background: before he met Lloyd Webber, he was a member of a rock group called the Aardvarks.

The first Rice and Lloyd Webber collaboration was a rather frail musical version of the life of philanthropist Dr Thomas Barnardo. Then, in 1967, came a commission to write a song for a newspaper's Girl of the Year contest. This song, and the girl, had their 15 minutes of fame, then faded away. Several other attempts at hit compositions also fell by the wayside, until Tim Rice observed that a song always seemed to have a better chance of success if it mentioned an American place name. The two laboured over an offering that began: 'I love a Kansas morning, Kansas mist at my window'. Alas, it was never sung, and went into a drawer to await a possible future airing.

Despite a lukewarm beginning, the team of Rice and Lloyd Webber was getting into its stride. In 1968 the pair dreamed up a 15-minute cantata for junior schoolboys. This joyous and funny version of the Old Testament tale of Joseph and his many-coloured coat was an enormous success and years later was expanded into a full musical. *Joseph and the Amazing Technicolor Dreamcoat* became the first paving stone in a glittering road.

Not the least influence on their fortunes was the support of New Zealand-born Martin Sullivan, the Dean of St Paul's Cathedral, who saw the original *Joseph* and liked it so much that he organised a performance at the cathedral in November 1968. By now the piece had been expanded to 35 minutes in length. No rarefied philosopher, Sullivan was an approachable and down-to-earth cleric: when he was notified that he was to be Dean of St Paul's, he went and bought an ice cream to celebrate. Sullivan found nothing to shock him in the pop rhythms of Lloyd Webber, or the way Rice had transformed the Old Testament into cheeky and idiomatic verse. Later, when the composers turned their attention to a more prominent biblical character, Sullivan's support would become vital.

But even growing fame and praise from the Dean of St Paul's didn't necessarily fill an empty bank account. Hope dawned for Lloyd Webber and Rice when two smart businessmen offered

Andrew Lloyd Webber and Tim Rice were not the first to make an oratorio about the biblical figure of Joseph. Handel had done it long before in the 1744 oratorio, 'Joseph and His Brothers'.

them a contract. The deal was a living wage for three years, and the businessmen would own 25 per cent of anything the pair composed within that period. This solved the problems of rent and food but Lloyd Webber and Rice felt impelled to come up with something better than the modest success that had attended the short Joseph oratorio. They went to visit Dean Martin Sullivan, who advised them to 'Have a look at the New Testament'.

While they were considering possible subjects, two influential events occurred. The rock musical *Hair*, first seen in New York in 1967, opened the following year on Broadway and in London. Clearly, rock music could function in the 'real world' of theatre and serious money. Even more significant was the ruckus caused by John Lennon who, in 1966, had created an international sensation by claiming that the Beatles were more popular than Jesus. Even in the liberal 1960s, the name of Jesus was still hot. Maybe, Tim Rice reasoned, Jesus could be a better box office drawcard than people thought; perhaps the Bible was indeed worth a second try.

In later years, the title *Jesus Christ Superstar* seemed immediately to conjure up the name Andrew Lloyd Webber but it may well be that lyricist Tim Rice provided the actual idea for an oratorio/opera on the last days of Jesus. Rice was obsessed with people who lived short, world-changing lives – John F. Kennedy, Robin Hood, Richard the Lionheart, even Hitler. Around 1969, Jesus and Judas joined that list.

Inspired by a magazine photo of Tom Jones, captioned 'Superstar', Lloyd Webber and Rice put together a song with the same title. Sung by the character of Judas, about Jesus, the song demanded an answer to the question, who was this Jesus? It was recorded by singer Murray Head and released late in 1969.

Again, Dean Martin Sullivan approved both of the recording and of the general idea. Rock music allied with two young male biblical figures, neither of them milksops, seemed to him a possible way of letting the Passion of Jesus reach a wider, younger audience. 'Please try to take Jesus down from a stained glass window,' he told Rice and Lloyd Webber. In a similar vein, the Chaplain to the Royal College of Music felt that biblical stories were too frequently sanitised and homogenised, and that biblical characters should be depicted as real people. An earthy treatment, rather than a lofty one, could deliver a serious message.

It was unlikely, however, that much useful religious fervour, or income, could be generated by just one song. But the company which had recorded the single suggested that a full-length work, based on the three-minute song 'Superstar', might be interesting. In fact they made a definite offer: a double LP recording about Jesus and Judas in musical form.

For Tim Rice and Andrew Lloyd Webber this was crunch time. In December 1969 they left London for a remote snowy village with the unlikely name of Stoke Edith, took rooms in a little hotel, read Fulton Sheen's *The Life of Christ* and set to work. In January 1970, the first draft emerged. The Bible was being converted into hard rock.

Word about the unusual project was already spreading. John Lennon let it be known that he was willing to consider playing the Jesus role, when the recording began, but he wanted Yoko Ono as Mary Magdalene. Lloyd Webber somehow deflected any formal discussion on the matter by publicly emphasising that the new work was an opera. No more was heard about Miss Ono.

But even without John Lennon or Yoko Ono, the project was advancing, and the work's structure needed a big ballad for the character of Mary Magdalene. Lloyd Webber looked into his bottom drawer, and came out with the forgotten 1967 pop song about Kansas. The first line became:

> I don't know how to love him
> What to do, how to move him.

Later, the tune was described by cynics as being 'inspired by', for which read 'stolen from', the slow movement of the Mendelssohn violin concerto. Nevertheless, when equipped with its new words, the song sounded like money, even in distant Stoke Edith.

The first version of the full *Jesus Christ Superstar* was recorded early in 1970, with Murray Head as Judas, Ian Gillan as Jesus and Barry Dennan as Pilate. On a night out in London, Andrew Lloyd Webber heard a previously unknown singer named Yvonne Elliman. A Hawaiian, of Irish, Japanese and Chinese ancestry, Elliman was an appealing beauty with an attractive, seductive voice. She became Mary Magdalene.

When the work was released as a record album later in 1970, it caused a sensation. *Time* proclaimed:

> It rivals the St John and St Matthew Passions of Bach, but manages to wear
> its underlying seriousness lightly. This may enrage the devout, but ought to

intrigue and perhaps inspire the agnostic young. *Superstar* provides the first real proof that rock can deal with a major subject on a broad symphonic or operatic scale.

The album sold in vast quantities, a million copies a month in the initial rush. Enter impresario Robert Stigwood, who had a bizarre idea: why not put it on the stage?

Yvonne Elliman, Andrew Lloyd Webber's original Mary Magdalene.

This was a prospect nobody had seriously considered, in spite of the obvious fact that the concept of *Jesus Christ Superstar* seemed more like an opera than an oratorio.

But by the time Stigwood secured the rights to stage it, the same notion had occurred to others. Fifteen pirate production companies had sprung up, and each had to be stymied by court orders to stop it presenting *Superstar* on stage. In the meantime, to advertise his own production, Stigwood organised the creation of *Superstar* badges, buttons, T-shirts, underwear and bikinis.

Besides such marketing gimmicks, the actual preparation for transforming *Superstar* from a recording into a stage show was enormous. Music had to be redrafted and repositioned, casting was a nightmare and Stigwood's somewhat extravagant ideas completely obliterated any traditional notions of simple Nazarene carpenters and peasant folk in smocks. In the stage production, one of Jesus's robes cost $20,000.

Jesus Christ Superstar opened on Broadway on 12 October 1971, with $1 million in advance bookings. American reaction among Christians was more pronounced than those in Britain. Indeed, as *Time* had predicted, the devout were enraged, and considerable opposition was mounted to the very idea of Jesus on a stage singing gospels in rock rhythm. Fortunately, there was equal support from those who thought that a new musical rhythm wouldn't do Jesus any harm, and the production went ahead.

When the show opened in Paris, the French producers insisted that Jesus actually be surrounded by stained glass windows, somewhat in negation of Martin Sullivan's early plea to the composers. But Mary Magdalene's ballad especially suited the French language: 'Je Ne Sais Pas Lui Aimer' regularly stopped the show.

The London opening was in August 1972. Critics were occasionally waspish – 'electronic gospel' – but their opinions were lost in the overwhelming public response. The London production of *Jesus Christ Superstar* went on to play for eight years. When the show reached the Southern Hemisphere, respected music critic Linden Saunders wrote in the *New Zealand Herald*:

> the show carries an immense impact, and comes with a meteoric force, not so much an entertainment as an experience. To label *Superstar* as pop is to do it less than justice; this is true rock opera. Webber has made a valid and powerful account of the Passion, using the music of his time. This is not musical heresy; indeed, it is the highest level of dramatic inspiration.

The government of Israel agreed to financial involvement in a movie of *Superstar*, to be shot in an Israeli desert. Somewhat to the chagrin of Rice and Lloyd Webber, the movie had some verbal rewrites by Melvyn Bragg, and its music supervised by André Previn. On a Mediterranean lecture cruise at the time the movie came out, Martin Sullivan once again found himself called to the defence. According to his widow he 'spent the entire time from Greece to Southampton with radio messages, settling a lot of people who were very angry about it'.

But worldwide, the success on stage and on record was gigantic. In view of this, Rice and Lloyd Webber's earlier biblical trifle about Joseph was resurrected. Although it had been written before *Superstar*, the recorded cantata of *Joseph and the Amazing Technicolor Dreamcoat*, now expanded, was artfully marketed as a follow-up show. Eventually a full-length show, *Joseph* has been staged all over the world.

Rice's lyrics for Mary Magdalene's big song trod gently the well-worn path about Mary as a woman formerly of easy virtue. Her song revealed that she has 'had so many men before' but she now had been 'changed'. Yvonne Elliman sang the role of Mary Magdalene on the original *Superstar* album and also in the New York stage production and in the movie. Her recording of 'I Don't Know How to Love Him' became a major hit, followed closely by Helen Reddy's version. After *Superstar*, Elliman continued singing and recording, finding another hit in the Bee Gees' 'If I Can't Have You' from *Saturday Night Fever*. Soon after, she retired from a musical career to marry and raise a family.

In the meantime, Tim Rice and Andrew Lloyd Webber were focusing their attention on another influential figure who had lived life in the fast lane and died young: an illegitimate Argentinean peasant, born Maria Ibarguren, who became known to the world as Evita Peron. And another million dollars was on its way.

Rudolph the Red-nosed Reindeer

Had a very shiny nose.

ROBERT MAY, JOHNNY MARKS, 1949

Because the legend of Santa Claus originates from Turkey, there would not have been any reindeer involved in the life of the real St Nicholas. But over the 1800 years since his death, the austere Bishop Nicholas from Turkey gradually became reinvented as a jolly gift-giver. In 1822 American poet Clement Moore wrote the poem 'A Visit from St Nicholas', better known as 'Twas the Night before Christmas', which nailed the image for all time – and gave St Nicholas a sleigh with eight reindeer: Dasher, Dancer, Prancer, Vixen, Comet, Cupid, Donner and Blitzen. Some 120 years later, a ninth reindeer emerged.

Clement Moore's poem never used the term Santa Claus, but it coincided with awareness in 18th-century New York that in Christmas street parades Dutch immigrants were honouring an unfamiliar figure, a man dressed in bishop's mitre, red robes and crook. This was St Nicholas – Sint Nikolas or, in the old style, Sinte Klaas.

By 1773 American journalists were reporting this as 'St. A. Claus' and in 1809 Washington Irving referred to him as 'Sinterklaas'. Then along came Moore's evocative poem, with its image of a jolly old man dressed in fur, dispensing toys from a sack, and urging his reindeer to hurry. This gradually merged with Sinte Klaas and resulted in the first known drawing of 'Santa Claus' in 1848 – jacketed, booted, hooded and in fur.

In 'The Twelve Days of Christmas', when the original term 'colly birds' began to cause confusion, it was gradually replaced by 'calling birds', though this is equally meaningless. In fact 'colly' is related to the world colliery, a coalmine, so it signifies something blackened as if by coal dust. Hence a colly bird is a blackbird.

In truth, back in the fourth century, St Nicholas was bishop of Myra (now called Demla) in the land we know as Turkey. But he was associated with gift giving: a statue in Demla shows him with two children and a sackful of presents.

Over time, Moore's depiction of an elfin St Nicholas image, with equally miniature reindeer, was brushed aside. Interested organisations wanting to make money out of this new Santa Claus figure needed to dress someone in the festive costume, but couldn't comply with Moore's notion of someone very small. Santa would have to become human size. He grew to be a financial phenomenon too. Promoted heavily in English-speaking countries, Santa Claus became so dominant that some people protested that he had replaced Jesus as the central figure of Christmas celebrations.

In 1939, with Santa Claus well established, a man called Robert May was living in Chicago, writing some Christmas advertising material for the big American retail chain, Montgomery Ward. One of the things he wrote was a feel-good poem about an unglamorous reindeer with a red nose, who was to be the ninth reindeer in Santa's team, and was called Rollo. When May submitted the poem to Montgomery Ward for consideration as part of their Christmas advertising, they didn't like the name Rollo. May tried Reginald, but that didn't go down well either. Then his young daughter suggested Rudolph and the Montgomery Ward executives said yes.

The poem was printed as a small colouring book that was included in every Christmas

Johnny Marks, who made a hit song out of Robert May's poem about a reindeer with a red nose.

purchase at their stores. In the 10 years that this was done, an estimated 10 million copies were given away. Rudolph attracted the attention of a cartoon maker and in 1944 he starred in a short animated movie. But the big development came in 1949. Robert May had a brother-in-law called Johnny Marks who, a decade after Rudolph was created, sat down and set the poem to a tune. It could have languished but a miracle occurred. The singing cowboy Gene Autry decided to record the song. The result was a sensation. Rudolph was both an ugly duckling and a Cinderella, albeit with four feet, and the public loved him. Gene Autry's recording of 'Rudolph the Red-Nosed Reindeer' went on to sell 50 million copies.

In 1964 a TV special was made, with Burl Ives as narrator, enlarging the story to show Rudolph's attraction to a lady reindeer called Clarice, and the adventures which befell them. In 1998 there was a full-length feature movie.

Rudolph has become such an accepted part of Christmas that it is hard to imagine December without him. In terms of the festival's religious heritage, he has no place at all, but in the fictional folklore created initially by the combination of one poem and the star power of Gene Autry, Rudolph is now right up there with the Star of Bethlehem.

A mondgreen is a misheard song lyric. One example is the person who for years thought that Santa had a reindeer called Olive, because of the way she heard 'All of the other reindeer' as 'Olive the other reindeer, used to laugh and call him names'.

Galway Bay

If you ever go across the sea to Ireland.

'Galway Bay' is one of the most beautiful songs ever written about a place, but the subtle inclusion of political statement nearly prevented its becoming a world-famous recording.

Its composer, Arthur Colahan, was born in Enniskillen, Ireland, in 1884. He was educated in Limerick and then attained an arts degree from University College, Dublin. His studies changed to medicine, and he graduated from Queen's College, Galway, in 1913. Throughout his university career he was known as a lively debater and a writer of original songs. The First World War found him in the British Army Medical Corps, serving in India. After 1918 Dr Colahan moved to Leicester in England, and became part of the medical services attached to that district's police and prisons.

Living and working away from his homeland, in a country regarded by many Irish as 'foreign', Colahan was often homesick for Ireland. He retained strong links with his family there, and returned frequently to visit his brothers and sisters. In the evenings he would take to the piano and the Colahan siblings would join in for an Irish singalong. Often, he would sing them songs of his own composition. He had maintained his interest in composing songs, and produced several still-popular favourites, including 'Macushla Mine', 'Cade Ring' and 'The Kylemore Pass'.

About 1927, Colahan wrote the words and music of what became his most famous song. It was motivated by his general sadness at being away from Ireland and focused on Galway Bay, where one of his brothers had earlier drowned. It was a song born of exile, with an attractive tune and pleasantly optimistic lyrics, and just a quiet undercurrent of melancholy.

Colahan viewed his music as a hobby and was not committed to organising his output of original songs in a professional way. He played music and composed songs to entertain himself and his family and friends. Often he didn't even write down his original material, since he was known to have an amazing memory and could summon almost any song he'd ever heard without resorting to notes on paper. For these reasons, 'Galway Bay' remained in his private repertoire for 15 years before it was copyrighted and published.

But despite the song's obvious appeal, there was a small problem. Dr Colahan's attractive mix of national loyalty, Irish whimsy and charming imagery concealed a less than discreet sting.

There had been tension and enmity between Ireland and England for centuries, continuing even after the establishment of the Republic of Ireland in 1921. Acknowledging this, the original words of 'Galway Bay' mentioned the English by name. The women digging praties (potatoes) were speaking a language the English did not know. And following that came a clear reference to the English coming and trying to teach 'their ways'. But the song gently dismissed any attempts to assimilate Irish culture into English – they might as well have tried 'to light a penny candle from a star'.

This was all very well, in an all-Irish context, but when the song reached radio broadcast level, discreet rewording was felt to be in order. After all, the composer lived in England himself, and things had moved on somewhat since 1927, when the words were first put down. The song's mention of the English led to a high-level decision when Bing Crosby decided to record 'Galway Bay' in 1947. Political correctness is normally only of very faint interest to a recording company but it was felt that cocking a snook at the English could be a liability on the international market. Crosby settled for a euphemism and the word 'strangers' was substituted for 'English'.

Although no evidence remains, it has to be assumed that since Arthur Colahan was still alive, aged only 63, he must have known of and approved the alteration. He was sufficiently sophisticated to have taken legal redress and perhaps even have Crosby's watered-down reading banned. But the Crosby recording achieved worldwide success and remained a bestseller for many years. A 1947 reregistering of the copyright included the word 'strangers' and it is a rare performance of 'Galway Bay' that uses the original 'English'. In Ireland the Crosby euphemism was widely known to be a substitute for the original reference, but it was nevertheless cheerfully accepted, on the grounds that the song did nothing but good for Ireland – and anyway, everybody in Ireland knew that 'the strangers' meant 'the English' so no real harm had been done.

Simultaneously with the record's release, sheet music, with a Bing Crosby cover portrait, was issued and 'Galway Bay' became known to millions. But Arthur Colahan made little or no attempt to bask in or capitalise on any glory. He was said to be humble about his achievement, and simply went on with his daily work. A month before he died, in 1952, 'Galway Bay' was included in the highly successful movie, *The Quiet Man*, starring John Wayne and Maureen O'Hara, but the movie's credits acknowledged only the song's arranger, Victor Young, with no mention of Arthur Colahan.

Another lack of acknowledgement occurred after Colahan's death. His body was returned to Ireland for burial but there had been some ill feeling with his estranged wife and his in-laws which somehow resulted in his being buried with scant ceremony and anonymously. The composer of one of the world's best-loved songs was buried in Galway Cemetery with a Celtic cross on his grave, but no name.

Romantic Galway Bay, Ireland.

As the old saying would have it, imitation is the sincerest form of flattery, and since the Crosby version of 'Galway Bay' there have been many variations on the verses – comic, satirical, cheeky and sometimes bawdy. Arthur Nicholas Colahan single-handedly brought more publicity to the district of Galway than anyone before or since. And, in doing so, he left the world a song as immortal as the bay itself.

I Could Have Danced All Night

And still have begged for more.

ALAN JAY LERNER, FREDERICK LOEWE, 1956

Unlikely though it seems, when Eliza Doolittle sings that she could have danced all night, she is the modern version of a legend that dates from several centuries before Christ. Eliza's ancient ancestor was a statue made of ivory, brought to life not by mastering 'the rain in Spain stays mainly in the plains' but by sacrificing cows with gilded horns.

The legend tells of Pygmalion, King of Cyprus in ancient times. The bachelor monarch, an expert sculptor, whiled away the time by carving a life-size statue of a beautiful woman. Some versions say it was carved in marble; other versions say it was made of pure white ivory. Although he was unimpressed by the wiles of real females, a strange yearning grew in the misogynist king that the statue should come to life and be his love.

Some time during the first century BC, the story was recounted by the Roman poet Ovid in his epic *Metamorphoses*. Ovid depicted Pygmalion as becoming totally lovelorn. The king ran his fingers over the statue, wishing it were flesh. He kissed the cold lips, and imagined them returning his kiss. He sang to the cold figure, laid gifts at its feet, hung it with jewels, embraced it and was convinced the 'woman' softened at his touch.

But the king wanted more. Fired with desire, Pygmalion prayed vehemently to Venus and sacrificed white heifers whose horns had been covered with gold, asking that his ice-cold beauty be given life. And Venus granted his prayer. The veins within the statue began to throb, the statue grew warm, its eyes opened and saw the man who had caused her to have life – and Pygmalion embraced his now-living love.

The statue's rise to love and a throne has many echoes elsewhere. The Bible tells of poor Esther, who became Queen of Persia. The slightly similar story of Cinderella, the poor girl who found happiness, riches and rank, has its origins in the ancient Orient. Charles Perrault's 1679 retelling of *Cinderella* is the most famous: the kitchen wench who went to the palace in a coach and slippers made of fur (mistakenly translated into English as 'glass').

But Ovid's *Metamorphoses* tale of Pygmalion persisted, albeit in slightly changing forms. Several centuries after Ovid, the story appeared in English in John Marston's erotic poem *Metamorphosis of Pigmalion's Image* (1598) and then again in William Morris's 1868–70 poem, *The Earthly Paradise*. As it passed through various literary forms, the story gained variations. Intrigued by the theme, in 1871 playwright W. S. Gilbert, of Gilbert and Sullivan fame, wrote *Pygmalion and Galatea*, about a married man whose wife is jealous of a statue her husband appears to fancy. But it was George Bernard Shaw's version, the 1912 play called simply *Pygmalion*, that outstripped all the others in popular appeal, and even more so when music was added over 40 years later.

Love never entered Shaw's play, in the sense of King Pygmalion's feelings for his statue. Henry Higgins' 'sculpture' was the recreation of a young woman from Cockney poverty to high-society salon perfection. Shaw was adamant that there should be no 'traditional' union of the play's two main characters.

Mrs Patrick Campbell, the original Eliza Doolittle in 1914, disagreed. Nearly 50 at the time, and playing an 18-year-old, Mrs Campbell was a star and a force to reckon with. Legend persists that she was not the first choice for the role but that other younger actresses had declined to say Shaw's line 'not bloody likely'. Stella Campbell caused a sensation when, as Eliza, she said the word 'bloody' onstage – considered outrageous at the time. But also, having left the set of Higgins' house in the final moments of the show, to Shaw's dismay she walked back onstage just as the curtain was falling, showing the audience that Eliza *had* returned.

The 1938 movie of Shaw's play, which won an Academy Award for best screenplay, also hinted at the end that Higgins and Eliza were not permanently separated. Film-maker Gabriel Pascal held the screen rights to the play, and formed the idea of making it into a musical. He suggested this to Rodgers and Hammerstein, who tried, then gave up and said no – and they weren't the only ones. Eventually, Alan Jay Lerner and Frederick Loewe said yes. They later discovered that they'd been virtually the last on a long list of others who'd turned the job down.

The original 'Fair Lady'. Julie Andrews as Eliza Doolittle, who 'could have danced all night'.

It was clear to Lerner and Loewe that the story of Shaw's *Pygmalion* was not a love story, and that the hero and the heroine did not finish up in each other's arms. For them, the central drama of the piece focused on the sadness of a brilliant man with all manner of skills, except social graces and the ability to love. Somewhat like King Pygmalion, and like George Bernard Shaw himself, Henry Higgins was a man who found it easier to be acerbic than to show affection.

Rex Harrison took a great deal of persuading to play the part. Apart from a notable ability to love ladies, he had never sung a note in public. Bit by bit the duo of Lerner and Loewe created 'songs' well ahead of time, for Harrison to approve and practise.

Lerner and Lowe took the first draft of several of their songs to Broadway icon Mary Martin. Although 40 at the time, Mary Martin had definite star status and one of her greatest successes, *The Sound of Music,* was still to come. Alas, the meeting did not go well. Afterwards Martin's husband told Lerner and Loewe that his wife had remarked what a shame it was that Lerner and Loewe had lost their talent.

Nineteen-year-old Julie Andrews was less of a problem. Lerner, who saw her in the New York production of *The Boy Friend,* reported in his autobiography, *On the Street Where I Live,* that 'the moment she set foot on stage, one could see she fairly radiated with some indefinable substance which is the difference between a talent and a star'. And her singing ability was in no doubt at all.

Lerner and Loewe composed material in the opposite way to Gilbert and Sullivan: Loewe wrote the tune first and Lerner fitted words to it. Visiting London, they wandered the real Covent Garden flower markets at 4 a.m. in winter, and heard genuine Cockneys using their colourful patois and inserting one word inside another like 'abso-bloody-lutely'. They also saw costermongers warming themselves around a charcoal brazier. All of this came out in their opening song to 'set' the character of Eliza. 'Wouldn't it Be Loverly?', a gentle number filled with foot-tapping optimism. Everybody was happy with it.

But as Higgins' 'songs' grew in effectiveness, and Stanley Holloway as Alfred Doolittle was clearly going to bring the house down, Lerner and Loewe felt the need for another showcase number for Julie Andrews. They felt that the right place for it would be after Eliza had conquered the line 'the rain in Spain stays mainly in the plain'. Six songs were written, then discarded, and still inspiration hadn't come for a showcase number. A week before formal rehearsals began, Alan Jay Lerner had an idea – the simple phrase 'I Could Have Danced All Night'. He passed on the suggested title to

Frederick Loewe, who seized upon it and fashioned a tune in a single day. Lerner added the lyrics within the next 24 hours. Julie Andrews now had her key number.

The song combined the required element of triumph that she had conquered the difficult vowels but also contained a subtle hint that part of the pleasure was in pleasing Higgins. The ambiguous quality of the lyrics shows the genius of Lerner's writing and the respect he paid to Shaw's original 'non-love-story', at least, at that point in the musical. 'I Could Have Danced All Night' is widely accepted as a quasi-love song, but this is not necessarily so. Eliza tells us that her spirits are high and she could have kept on dancing – it is a song of achievement. The listener assumes that her heart has taken flight because of being held in Higgins' arms but this isn't stated. He is briefly alluded to, but only as a catalyst for her wish to keep on dancing. There is an indication that she feels that Higgins is something more than just a teacher, but the words are distinctly ambiguous. But whatever may have inspired Eliza to dance all night, Higgins demonstrates his own apparent indifference to her by announcing that he danced with her at the ball simply to get her away from the scrutiny of Zoltan Karpathy, the hairy hound from Budapest.

Later in the show, producers realised that Eliza's entrance at the ball in a beautiful gown was not having the required impact, simply because all the other women in the ball scene were beautifully dressed too. A scene was added earlier, where she appeared at the top of the stairs in Higgins' house dressed for the ball, and made a stately descent while the orchestra played 'I Could Have Danced All Night'. They got their impact.

My Fair Lady opened on Broadway in March 1956. Besides Julie Andrews, Rex Harrison and Stanley Holloway, veteran beauty Cathleen Nesbitt played Higgins' mother, and 5000 singer-dancers had auditioned for the 16 chorus places. The show was a solid-gold packed-out hit. Immediately the cast album was recorded, bootleg copies started flying out of the United States like migrating locusts, as ship and air stewards, tourists and families with overseas relatives despatched dozens of copies to places where the record wasn't yet on sale. Julie Andrews could be heard singing 'I Could Have Danced All Night' all over Britain, the Continent, South America and the South Pacific. In the United States where it *was* officially on sale, the *My Fair Lady* original cast album stayed at No. 1 for two years. In spite of the overwhelming success, Alan Jay Lerner confessed to being haunted by Mary Martin's remark, which she must have lived to regret, that he and Frederick Loewe had lost their talent.

George Bernard Shaw had written a prose epilogue to *Pygmalion* explaining why Eliza did not, and could not, marry Higgins, and had instead married Freddy Eynsford-Hill. The theatre-going public most emphatically did not want to know this. In musical theatre tradition, the prince and the goose girl must finish the show hand-in-hand. In *My Fair Lady* this doesn't actually happen, but Lerner and Lowe had bowed to the massive public desire that Eliza's dramatic departure from Higgins' house was followed, if only for a few seconds, by her ultimate return before the curtain came down.

Inevitably, discussion about a film version began. Peter O'Toole was considered for Higgins. So, briefly, was Rock Hudson. The role was offered to Cary Grant, who is reputed to have said, 'Not only will I not do it, but if Rex Harrison doesn't play the role I won't even go and see it.' It had to be Rex Harrison. And Eliza? A film studio wanted a guaranteed film name, which Julie Andrews at that time was not. English-born Elizabeth Taylor, then 32, was interested in playing the role, but couldn't sing well enough. Belgian-born 35-year-old Audrey Hepburn was no singer either but she had a vulnerability and bankability that appealed to the money men.

The resulting movie was a huge success, slightly soured, in the opinion of many, by the absence of Julie Andrews, and the knowledge that Audrey Hepburn wasn't actually singing. She wanted to, and recorded most of the soundtrack, but, as Lerner wrote, 'Audrey Hepburn can sit in a control room, listen to a sadly inadequate voice, and somewhere between the inner ear and the cortex, convert it into Joan Sutherland.' Some of Hepburn's *sprechgesang* (speaking-cum-singing) was retained but invisible soprano Marni Nixon was brought in to provide the rest, including the top G at the end of 'I Could Have Danced All Night'.

'I Could Have Danced All Night' became the most popular song Lerner and Loewe every composed together. Sales of *My Fair Lady* cast albums have sold nearly 20 million, and dozens of artists have recorded the song, including hit versions from Dinah Shore, Johnny Mathis, Peggy Lee and Frank Sinatra (who managed to avoid the final top G). Classic cellist Yo Yo Ma offered his instrumental version, as did several orchestras, and opera divas Birgit Nilsson, Renée Fleming, Kiri Te Kanawa and Angela Gheorghiu have all at once let their 'heart take flight' without any fear of the top G.

In London during the 1950s, TV director Douglas Drury's flatmate Desmond Digby was a student at the Slade School of Art. A fellow student of Digby's was Tony Walton, who had been Julie Andrews' sweetheart for several years, and who was a frequent visitor to the Drury–Digby flat. Walton and Julie corresponded by sending sound tapes to each other, and Walton was expecting Julie to finish *The Boy Friend* in New York and be home in London by Christmas. One Friday night Walton was gloomy: 'She's not coming just yet. She's moving into another show – a musical version of Shaw's *Pygmalion*.' Douglas Drury said reassuringly, 'She'll be back soon. That will never work.'

Then the days dwindle down to a precious few.

In 1933 the Jewish German composer Kurt Weill and his wife Lotte Lenya escaped the tyranny of Hitler's dictatorship and, after two years in Paris, went to the United States, where they settled in 1937. Weill's writing partnership with Bertolt Brecht had been particularly successful with *The Threepenny Opera* and its major hit song 'Mack The Knife', sung by Lenya.

With American writer Maxwell Anderson, Kurt Weill discussed the idea of a play or musical built around the story of New York's history. They looked at *Father Knickerbocker's History Of New York* by Washington Irving and decided that yes, a musical was possible. Its title was *Knickerbocker Holiday*. Movie star Walter Huston was engaged to play the character of Pieter Stuyvesant, the real-life Governor of New Amsterdam, as New York was originally known. To *act* the governor – nobody had any plans for him to sing. Huston, however, thought otherwise, and pronounced that he, as Stuyvesant ('an old bastard'), should have at least one moment where he could stop being domineering and show some charm to a pretty young woman.

Dismayed, Anderson and Weill sat together to create a more-or-less love song which could be sung to somebody young by somebody old – and by a man whose singing ability was completely unknown. Pre-dating *My Fair Lady* by 18 years, they developed an almost-spoken simple tune, with lyrics in a deliberately conversational style. They called it 'September Song'. Walter Huston, who was only 54, took to the song like a duck to water. His singing of 'September Song' was so charming that audiences became confused about whether Stuyvesant was good or bad. In the words of writer Robin Stummer, Huston sang the song 'like a grandfather doing a turn at a family reunion'.

The age-reminiscing-about-youth theme was played down by subsequent recording artists. Ella Fitzgerald and Sarah Vaughan gave it a torchy sound; Lou Reed gave an assertive take-it-or-leave-it interpretation. But Bing Crosby seemed to love the song. It was one of his earliest major hits, in 1943, and 34 years later he recorded it again, a month before he died. As the song decreed, Bing had run out of time for the waiting game.

Blue Moon

You saw me standing alone.

RICHARD RODGERS, LORENZ HART, 1934

In general, the expression 'blue moon' indicates that something rare has happened, or might happen – and that there are long intervals between its occurrences. An actual blue moon might be only mythical, but the well-known song that commemorated this notion was more like a musical orphan, passed from family to family.

In 1933 Richard Rodgers and Lorenz Hart were engaged to write songs for an MGM movie called *Hollywood Party*, which was being planned as an extravaganza starring Clark Gable, Jean Harlow, Wallace Beery and Joan Crawford. An idea was advanced that in one scene, Harlow would appear as a young woman dreaming of becoming a Hollywood star.

This concept turned into a possible musical number and Rodgers and Hart created a song called 'The Prayer'. But vacillations and upheavals seemed to have surrounded the movie and in the process the four original stars were replaced by Jimmy Durante, Laurel and Hardy, Lupe Velez – and Mickey Mouse. Harlow never appeared and 'The Prayer' was not even recorded.

A year later, Rodgers and Hart created a title song for the movie *Manhattan Melodrama*, starring Clark Gable, William Powell, Myrna Loy, and a very young Mickey Rooney. As a title song for the new film, they decided to retain Rodgers' melody from 'The Prayer' but in a new guise with different lyrics from Hart. The song became 'It's Just That Kind of Play', a somewhat breathless commentary on gulping the morning coffee and catching the subway in Manhattan. But, again, it was dropped.

However, a nightclub scene later in the movie required a new song and Rodgers and Hart were asked to provide one. Richard Rodgers still had faith in his tune so long-suffering Lorenz Hart wrote a third set of lyrics, this time for a woman singing about men. The actress who sang it was a vivacious young blonde called Shirley Ross, who was required to sing Hart's new lyrics, 'The Bad in Every Man', in complete blackface. Although this did little for her career in terms of recognition, she did move on to some fame, and her voice can still be heard singing with Bob Hope in their classic debut broadcast, which introduced the songs 'Thanks for the Memory' and 'Two Sleepy People'.

It would have been a Cinderella story for Rodgers and Hart if this movie had made the song a hit. Alas, this was not so. The nightclub scene caused little stir, and the movie's main claim to fame was centred around the fact that when bank robber John Dillinger left a cinema after watching this film in July 1934 he was gunned to death on the street.

But the song's pillar-to-post routine wasn't quite finished. An executive in MGM's publishing department seemed to agree that the melody had a future. He suggested to Rodgers and Hart that if it could be revised into a newer, more romantic version, it could be published as a separate venture.

Lorenz Hart sat down and came up with the fourth version: 'Blue Moon, you saw me standing alone'. And finally, Cinderella made it to the ball and the song was published. At the time, radio entertainment was extremely important and 'Blue Moon' became the theme song for a popular programme called *Hollywood Hotel*. From then on it was a hit.

It wasn't that Rodgers and Hart needed a hit. Their breakthrough had come 10 years before, when a show called *Garrick Gaieties*, using all their songs, went on for a planned one-night show, and was so successful it ran for over a year. Before the Hollywood merry-go-round which resulted in 'Blue Moon', they had already composed for 16 musicals and five movies, and generated a multitude of hits, including 'Mountain Greenery', 'Thou Swell', 'With a Song in My Heart', 'Ten Cents a Dance' and 'Isn't it Romantic?'.

But a year after it was first heard, 'Blue Moon' was recorded by Connee Boswell, and its magic carpet began to fly. Following her, over the years, came stellar recordings by Frank Sinatra, Billie Holiday, Vaughan Munroe, Dean Martin, Frankie Laine, Bobby Vinton, Mel Tormé, Glenn Miller, Nat King Cole, Tommy Dorsey and Tony Bennett. There were also jazz treatments from Ella Fitzgerald, Louis Armstrong, Dizzy Gillespie and Django Reinhardt. A country version came from The Mavericks, and rock crossovers included performances by Elvis Presley, Eric Clapton, Bob Dylan, Rod Stewart and Sam Cooke.

In 1961 a male group called The Marcels had four tracks to record in a session, but the singers were stumped after they'd recorded the third track. One suggested 'Blue Moon', which he felt fairly sure he knew well enough to teach the others. The producer agreed, and after one hour's practice, The Marcels put down 'Blue Moon', with a doo-wop sound. The record was a sensation (one radio station played it 26 times in one day) and sold over a million copies. It is featured in the Rock and Roll Hall of Fame as one of the 500 songs which shaped rock'n'roll. The only person who didn't like it was the composer Richard Rodgers, who objected to the 'feel' of their version, and its bomp-baba-bomp introduction.

As a song, instrumental or incidental music, 'Blue Moon' has been heard in an impressive number of movies, associated with artists as disparate as the Marx Brothers and Elvis. Besides the song's original outing in Manhattan Melodrama, the melody – sometimes with words, sometimes without – can be heard in Malaya (sung by Valentina Cortesa), East Side/West Side, With a Song in My Heart (sung by Jane Froman), Rogue Cop, 8½, Viva Las Vegas, Words and Music, At the Circus, New York New York (sung by Robert de Niro), An American Werewolf in London, Selena, Flesh and Bone, The Adventures of Pluto Nash, Grease, Where the Heart Is, Four Friends, Rich in Love, Desert Hearts, Biloxi Blues, Catch Me If You Can, The Remains of the Day, Dante's Peak and Notting Hill.

Richard Rodgers and Lorenz Hart wrote some 38 professional shows and films between 1919 and 1943. After 'Blue Moon' came many more hits: 'Bewitched, Bothered and Bewildered', 'Falling in Love with Love', 'There's a Small Hotel', 'Johnny One Note', 'My Funny Valentine', 'This Can't Be Love' and 'The Lady is a Tramp'. The two continued working together until Hart's death, when Richard Rodgers worked with other lyricists, most notably Oscar Hammerstein II.

A common explanation of the expression 'blue moon' is that if two full moons appear in one calendar month, one of them is called a blue moon. But two full moons in one month isn't all that uncommon. And why the colour 'blue'?

The expression has been in the English language since 1528, when it was used in a sardonic way to refer to something which is never going to happen – the implication being that a blue moon is a ridiculous impossibility. That meaning still remains, in the (slightly modified) sense that if something is not impossible, it is nevertheless very rare.

It is far from clear what interpretation of 'blue moon' Rodgers and Hart had in mind when they created the scenario of the song. For the pedantically minded, there is a mild puzzle about what Lorenz Hart meant by this particular depiction of a blue moon. Certainly the one person in a million who claims to have seen an actual blue-ish moon, never claims to have seen it change back to gold in the blink of an eye.

Hart could have been using 'blue' in its sense of being sad and downhearted – a lonely person without even a dream. Or, if the song is seen as referring to an incident in the past, it could be that the singer is telling us of a visit from good fortune which is very unexpected, even unlikely, positively rare! So it must have happened 'under a blue moon'.

But whatever inspired Rodgers and Hart to choose the image, it didn't affect the colour of the money it bought in. Like the moon in the lyrics, the song turned to gold.

You Made Me Love You

I didn't want to do it.

JAMES MONACO, JOSEPH McCARTHY, 1913

Al Jolson sang it, Fanny Brice sang it, but when Judy Garland sang it to a photograph of Clark Gable a whole new audience tuned in. During the early years of the 20th century, funny lady Fanny Brice's vaudeville act included 'You Made Me Love You'. She sang the first verse and chorus quite straight – lovelorn and serious. But when she reached the second verse, the true Fanny Brice broke through, and the presentation got funnier and funnier.

At much the same time, Al Jolson was also singing it – and creating a gimmick. His first ever blackface appearance was in a 1913 New York show, *Honeymoon Express*. Jolson played a character called Gus, and sang 'You Made Me Love You', which didn't belong to the show, but had been published that same year, and was interpolated. Because of a painful ingrown toenail, Jolson went down on one knee to sing and opened his arms wide, both for balance and to 'embrace' the whole audience. The stance became a trademark and the song was a regular Jolson offering for the rest of his career. Thirty-three years after his first performance, he sang it on the soundtrack of the movie, *The Jolson Story*.

A little over a decade after Jolson and Fanny Brice had sung 'You Made Me Love You', a child joined her family's vaudeville act. Just past her second birthday, Frances Gumm sang her first solo on stage, and as she grew, so did her rich and expressive voice.

Throughout her childhood, her mother would stage her appearances so that the child was sitting heavily draped on top of a piano, with a tiny spotlight just on her face. At the finish of her song, the light would widen, she would abandon the huge shawl and step off the piano, astonishing the audience that this 'woman's' voice they had just heard was coming from a diminutive pre-teen child.

Frances Gumm didn't like her first name, but she liked a Hoagy Carmichael song about a girl called Judy, with a voice as fresh as spring. And a vaudeville theatre had once mistakenly printed her surname as Glum, which put her right off Gumm. So a new surname evolved, using the surname of the *New York World-Telegram* critic, Robert Garland. And Frances Gumm was no more.

Judy Garland was contracted to Metro Goldwyn Mayer when she was only 13. Initially the administration was impressed with her spectacular voice, but beyond that, nobody knew quite what to do with her. She was not cute, like Shirley Temple, and she did not have the prettiness or pure soprano of her contemporary, Deanna Durbin. And she was too old for child roles and not old enough for romantic roles, even teenage ones. Sent out to sing on radio shows, she became experienced and admired, but still was not used in a real movie role. Louis B. Mayer, having hired her, more or less ignored

her. When she was 15, however, an unusual opportunity arose. It was not a film role, but a chance to remind the movers and shakers of Hollywood that she was still there – and that she was a very good singer.

Garland was booked to sing on a radio show hosted by Ben Bernie. She wanted to sing an Ethel Merman song, and she could, but her MGM pianist Roger Edens didn't agree. A child singing adult songs might have been okay as a vaudeville gimmick but it would not please the slightly more prim denizens of movie-making. So the pianist came up with an old 1913 song, 'You Made Me Love You', and suggested that it could be sung to the radio host as if by a teenage girl who had fallen in love with his style. Edens

Al Jolson. The kneeling was because of a painful toe.

constructed a new verse, beginning 'Dear Mr Bernie'. The two set to work learning it. Then, the day before the broadcast, fate stepped in.

MGM was staging a birthday party for one of its top stars, Clark Gable, known as the 'King.' Hollywood royalty would be there, and an MGM executive who had Judy Garland's interests at heart suggested to Louis Mayer that Judy should sing a song at the party, and this was agreed. Edens crossed out 'Dear Mr Bernie', wrote in Dear Mr Gable' and changed Judy Garland's life.

At the party, a glittering array of stars and executives toasted Gable and his cake and candles, and then the sound of a piano was heard. The lights came up on a 15-year-old girl who sang to Mr Gable that his movies made her heart go bang, and she had to write him a letter to let him know. When she got to the part about his brand of kisses being what she'd die for, Gable walked to the piano and kissed her. The guests were joyous. Louis Mayer took notice, and the King gave her a charm bracelet as a thank you. As a result of her successful party item, Garland was immediately placed in a concert the following night, starring those formidable talents Sophie Tucker and Eddie Cantor. She sang 'You Made Me Love You' and completely stole the show.

In the eyes of the movie-going world the defining performance of the song came in MGM's *Broadway Melody of 1939.* As the daughter of a boarding-house keeper, played by Sophie Tucker, Garland was seen alone in her room singing to a photo of Clark Gable propped up in front of her. From that moment on she was a star, and the song achieved classic status. For the next 30 years audiences demanded that Garland sing it, up to and including her final performances in 1969.

But Judy Garland, Fanny Brice and Al Jolson weren't the only ones to sing the song. In the 1920s and 1930s it was often sung by Ruth Etting, 'America's Sweetheart of Song', and Doris Day sang it in *Love Me Or Leave Me,* the 1955 film biography of Etting. Louis Armstrong had recorded it in 1926, and the song surfaced in the 1934 Victor McLaglen movie, *Wharf Angel.* Helen Forrest sang it in *Private Buckaroo* (1942) and in the same year it featured in *Syncopation* with Jackie Cooper and Connee Boswell. Harry James's band version had been a major success in 1941, and his next recording of it in 1946 was an even bigger success. Two years later Jeanette MacDonald sang it in *Three Daring Daughters* and Patsy Cline included it on her 1962 album, *Sentimentally Yours.*

The song seemed to cross many barriers. It can be heard in the Beatles movie, *Magical Mystery Tour,* as part of a slightly raffish singalong in the bus.

Silent Night

All is calm, all is bright.

FRANZ GRUBER, JOSEPH MOHR, 1818

For many years a charming story has been told about mice eating the leather bellows of an organ in the Austrian village of Oberndorf on Christmas Eve, 1818. So, with only a few hours to spare, the assistant priest Joseph Mohr and the organist Franz Gruber composed a Christmas song called 'Stille Nacht', which could be sung on Christmas Day, accompanied only by guitar.

At least two parts of the story have been revealed as fanciful – the mice, and the hurried creation of words and music – but it is certain that 'Silent Night' was first heard on Christmas Eve 1818 in the church of St Nicholas in Oberndorf, 20 kilometres north of Salzburg. (Oberndorf had been in Bavaria but that year had been redesignated as Austrian.) The song's composer, Franz Gruber, did eventually write down the story of how the song came into being, but he waited 30 years to do so.

He made no mention of mice, only that the church's organ was in a sad state of disrepair and the congregation couldn't afford to fix it. Mouse-holes in the leather? Maybe, but he didn't say so. And far from the song's words being written in the space of a few hours, scholars can show that Joseph Mohr, the 26-year-old priest, had written the words of 'Stille Nacht' as a poem two years earlier, when he was a priest in Mariapfarr. According to Gruber's account, Mohr walked from his room to the organist's house to ask if his poem could be set to music for the Christmas Eve midnight mass. He suggested that it feature two solo voices and the church choir, and be accompanied only by a guitar. That 20-minute walk led to the creation of a memorable song.

Franz Gruber was an accomplished musician. He composed nearly 100 other pieces and was accustomed to creating music for specific occasions. It is possible that he was not thrilled at the idea of composing for a guitar, which at that time was regarded as an instrument suited only to public bars and uninhibited gatherings. It was sometimes called 'the plucking violin'. But the real concern was that the traditional mass not be left without music.

So the first-ever performance of 'Silent Night' took place at midnight that Christmas Eve in 1818 with Mohr and Gruber as soloists. Both men were capable singers, Mohr played the guitar as well, and the choir joined in the last two lines of each verse. The villagers liked the song.

The following year, organ builder Carl Mauracher made various attempts to repair

Thousands visit the 'Silent Night Chapel' in Oberndorf, Austria, built in 1937 on the site of the original church where the song was first sung in 1818.

the faulty Oberndorf organ. On one of his visits he came across some music of 'Christmas Song' (it wasn't called 'Silent Night' until later), took it away with him and apparently passed it around. Soon choirs in the area were singing the song. Over the next decade it was heard, usually with choirs, as far away as Munich and Leipzig, and within 20 years was performed in New York, but without any acknowledgment of who had written it. In 1832 the 'Christmas Song' was first seen in print, when the publishing firm of Friese, Dresden and Leipzig included it in a book of 'genuine Tyrolean songs' and described it as 'of questionable origin'.

In their lifetime, neither Mohr nor Gruber was accorded much recognition for the simple but haunting song they had created. Mohr remained virtually unknown and when he died at the age of 56, as a priest in the town of Wagrain, he was so poor that the town had to pay for his funeral. Gruber had a colourful private life. A teacher as well as an organist, he was appointed to the position of another teacher who had died, and married his widow. When she died,

Gruber married a former pupil, and when she died too, Gruber married again. In the meantime, he had, perhaps understandably, almost forgotten about the melody he had composed in 1818. It took an inquiry from a king, more than three decades later, to remind him.

King Friedrich Wilhelm IV of Prussia noticed the music of 'Silent Night' in 1853 and although the music said that the composer was not known, he suspected it could have been Michael Haydn, the brother of Franz Joseph Haydn. Friedrich instructed an emissary to find the composer of the song. It took a year to track down Franz Gruber, now in his sixties and working as an organist in Hallein. The startled Gruber obeyed the royal command for information and wrote a letter, detailing as best he could, his memory of the song's creation. This was the first known explanation of the song's history.

The original German carol had six verses but only the first, second and sixth are generally sung in English:

Silent night, holy night!
All is calm, all is bright.
Round yon Virgin, Mother and Child.
Holy Infant, so tender and mild,
Sleep in heavenly peace,
Sleep in heavenly peace.

Silent night, holy night!
Shepherds quake at the sight.
Glories stream from Heaven afar,
Heavenly Hosts sing Alleluia,
Christ, the Saviour, is born!
Christ, the Saviour, is born.

Silent night, holy night!
Son of God, love's pure light.
Radiant beams from Thy holy face
With the dawn of redeeming grace,
Jesus, Lord, at Thy birth.
Jesus, Lord, at Thy birth.

The king had asked for the original score but Gruber didn't have it, so wrote one out from cloudy memory. Over the following years, he rewrote four or five other 'rememberings' of the song, all slightly different. This set in train all kinds of dispute and ill-feeling about 'corruption' of the treasured song, which persisted through many decades, including the Nazi era. The Fascists were uncomfortable about the song's simple Christianity and attempted to change the words. Fortunately, years later a copy of the original music, hand-written by Joseph Mohr, was discovered – for two voices, chorus and guitar, exactly as first performed. The music was accompanied by Mohr's own account, written shortly after the first performance, attributing the music to Gruber. Mohr's 'original' is now in the Carolinum Augusteum Museum in Salzburg.

Joseph Mohr was too insignificant and too poor ever to have been painted or drawn but by 1912 'Silent Night' had become so well known that the town of Wagrain decided to honour the priest in recognition of the now world-famous lyrics he had written. This honour would take the form of a bronze bust. By then, however, Mohr had been buried in the town church's graveyard for over 60 years and nobody could remember what he looked like. So his corpse was dug up and its skull removed. The planned bust never eventuated and the skull spent 25 years separated from the rest of Mohr's reburied skeleton. Eventually the skull was passed back to Oberndorf, where it was buried in the wall behind the Silent Night Memorial Chapel, in an unmarked spot.

The original Church of St Nicholas in Oberndorf where 'Silent Night' made its debut, was pulled down in 1906. A decade later, the foundation stone for a Silent Night Memorial Chapel was laid, and it opened in 1937. Thousands of visitors come to it each year, especially on Christmas Eve, when an evening service commemorating Joseph Mohr and Franz Gruber is held in the square adjoining the chapel. At the end of the service, 'Silent Night' is performed as written, with two soloists, a choir and guitar accompaniment. Then the visitors join in, all singing in their own language.

The town of Hallein near Salzburg, where composer Franz Gruber died, now has the Franz Xavier Gruber Museum, in his former home next to his grave. The museum contains exhibits concerning Gruber and 'Silent Night', in particular the actual guitar on which Joseph Mohr played the accompaniment for the song's first performance in 1818.

A version of 'Silent Night' in English was published in America in 1849. There have been many differing versions of Joseph Mohr's words in English, but the 1859 translation by the Reverend Freeman Young is the version usually heard. By some reckonings, 'Silent Night' has been translated into 300 languages and dialects, including 14 different versions in Latin. Recordings of the song are believed to have begun in 1905 with the Haydn Quartet, and continued through every musical context imaginable, from Burl Ives to the Vienna Boys' Choir, Ethel Smith on organ to Enya singing in Irish. One recording, perhaps not universally welcomed, features the song 'sung' by a cat called Jordy, accompanied by The Carol Cats. It is a triumph of the digital audio workstation skill, though not perhaps of good taste.

Despite the disputes about its origins, 'Silent Night' has become an aural anchor of Christmas. It is sung in cathedrals, on street corners, by formal choirs, at office parties, and by a wide range of singers from opera stars to Elvis. And you are as likely to hear it in South America, Hong Kong, Montreal or Outback Australia, as you are in Oberndorf.

Jingle Bells

'Jingle Bells' was composed for a children's church group concert and originally had no connection with Christmas, which is never mentioned during the song's four verses. Its title was 'One Horse Open Sleigh', and it was composed by American organist James L. Pierpont and published in 1857, then republished as 'Jingle Bells' two years later. It became popular for Christmas events and is now firmly associated with that time of year. It was first recorded in 1898 by a male quartet, and is now sung in many parts of the world, often by children who have no idea what a 'one-horse sleigh' could mean and who have never seen snow. 'Jingle Bells' was the first song Judy Garland ever sang in public, aged two and a half, accompanying herself with a little bell.

'Jingle Bells' may have been the first song broadcast from space. In December 1965 the Gemini 6 astronauts made a light-hearted broadcast, reporting that they had sighted a red-suited pilot in a 'module' with eight smaller 'modules' which appeared to be drawing it. They then produced a harmonica and some little bells, and sang 'Jingle Bells' to mission control.

One-Horse Open Sleigh (original words):

Dashing through the snow
In a one-horse open sleigh,
O'er the fields we go
Laughing all the way.
Bells on bobtail ring
Making spirits bright.
What fun it is to laugh and sing
A sleighing song tonight.

Chorus:
Jingle bells, jingle bells,
Jingle all the way;
Oh! what joy it is to ride
In a one-horse open sleigh.

A day or two ago
I thought I'd take a ride
And soon Miss Fanny Bright
Was seated by my side.
The horse was lean and lank,
Misfortune seemed his lot.
He got into a drifted bank
And then we got upsot. *

Chorus

A day or two ago,
The story I must tell.
I went out on the snow,
And on my back I fell.
A gent was riding by
In a one-horse open sleigh.
He laughed as there I sprawling lie,
But quickly drove away.

Chorus

Now the ground is white,
Go it while you're young.
Take the girls along
And sing this sleighing song.
Just get a bobtailed bay,
Two forty as his speed. **
Hitch him to an open sleigh
And crack! You'll take the lead.

Chorus

* 'Upsot': In some dialects means 'capsized'. Here it is possibly an old way of saying 'upset' in the sense of being 'overturned'.

** 'Two forty as his speed': Thought to describe a brisk pace for a harness-racing horse – a mile in two minutes and forty seconds.

Beyond the Blue Horizon

Waits a beautiful day.

Leo Robin, Richard A. Whiting, W. Franke Harling, 1930

At her peak, Jeanette MacDonald was one of the most famous film stars in the world. A superstar in the top 10 box-office earners, she topped magazine popularity polls, was named 'Queen of the Screen', drew crowds wherever she went and had sufficient clout to negotiate her career to her own advantage.

MacDonald had natural beauty, a light but attractive singing voice and a highly intelligent way with dialogue. But apart from film-friendly talents like these, she was hard-working and easy to publicise – always ready with a witty response to questions, not averse to a diva lifestyle and diligently performing live concerts. This encouraged fans of her films to see her in person, and vice versa.

There was also discreet acknowledgement among those in the know that her ingénue persona actually lived in harmony with a tough-minded woman of firm values and even firmer opinions, especially when it came to her own worth to the film industry. Hence her behind-the-scenes nickname, 'The Iron Butterfly', and Hollywood gossip queen Louella Parsons described her as 'the greatest showman in Hollywood'. But at least one highly publicised event in MacDonald's career had absolutely nothing to do with anything she had said or done. In fact the event never took place: it was only a rumour. But the legend it created lingered throughout the rest of her career. It arose because of the song 'Beyond the Blue Horizon'.

In August 1930, there was a car crash near Bruges in Belgium, and two people with injuries were taken to a nearby hospital. Their identity was concealed. Two days later, the man was spirited away in a private train. The woman was never seen in public. An instant rumour arose that the man was Crown Prince Umberto of Italy and, for no discernible reason, that the mysterious woman was film star Jeanette MacDonald. The rumours continued to spread, and magnify. It was whispered that MacDonald had gone to visit Charlie Chaplin in Juan-les-Pins and delivered to him, for safe keeping, love letters written to her by Prince Umberto. But these letters had found their way to the prince's father, King Victor Emmanuel III, who was so relieved to have them out of view that he signed a naval treaty with England. It was muttered that Prince Umberto's wife, Princess Marie-José of Belgium, had gone to the French Riviera and accosted MacDonald while she was filming the movie *Monte Carlo* there. And there was an extra *frisson* – that the feisty princess had flung sulphuric acid right into one of Hollywood's most beautiful faces.

And so the stories raged underground, and eventually above ground as well. Newspapers revealed that the mysterious couple was in fact a Spanish millionaire and his Italian girlfriend, who slightly resembled Jeanette MacDonald. But the Continental public would have none of it. Everyone had heard that MacDonald was now either scarred or dead, couldn't sing and her sister was standing in for her.

The key to the vague notion that Jeanette MacDonald was involved in all this was her latest film, *Monte Carlo*, and her delightful song 'Beyond the Blue Horizon'. But there was not a grain of truth in any version of the scandal, for the simple reason that Jeanette MacDonald had never set foot in Europe. All the filming of *Monte Carlo* was done in California, even the scene where she sang 'Beyond the Blue Horizon', sitting in a train, supposedly en route for the Riviera, with a clever musical arrangement that was almost a duet with the train noises – soprano plus whistles, clacking wheels and rhythmic engine noises. So convincing was the scene, as MacDonald waved to field workers seen through the train window, that Europeans refused to believe that the train was actually chugging through part of California.

There was talk of MacDonald's movies being banned, and a leading publication pointed out that France had given the United States a Statue of Liberty , but they did 'not expect a Statue of Indecency in return'. But Jeanette MacDonald was not called 'The Iron Butterfly' for nothing. It became clear to her that she must confront the situation by travelling to the Continent, and that she would perform a concert in Paris at the huge Empire Theatre. Armed with letters from the American State Department, documents, affidavits and fingerprinted identity papers, all proving she had never ever been in Europe before, she set sail for Le Havre. A media turmoil awaited her arrival.

Four hours of chaos ensued at the railway station. There was a press conference. Journalists behaved aloofly, suspicious that this woman, who had not yet sung, was her own non-singing sister, or some other impostor. Meanwhile supporters of Mussolini threatened to attack the theatre for her having humiliated the Italian royal family.

Having survived the press conference, Jeanette MacDonald, dressed in orange crepe de chine, drifted onto the stage of the Empire Theatre to an audience of 3000 and sang – in perfect French. The audience erupted. At the sound of that famous soprano voice, nobody dared say, 'That isn't her.' She addressed the audience in French. Refined, friendly and distinguished, MacDonald conquered even the cynics before her. Said a critic, 'She has the voice of a rose, if roses could sing.' The beautiful red-haired American had never even met the Italian royal family but the fictitious affair was replaced by a true and long-lasting romance between Jeanette MacDonald and France. (Rumours immediately began of a new involvement with Maurice Chevalier – another fabrication.)

Hollywood diva Jeanette MacDonald. She sang 'Beyond the Blue Horizon' sitting in a Californian train – not in Europe.

Eventually the royal rumour faded but 'Beyond the Blue Horizon' did not, and it became one of the most famous of Macdonald's songs. In the 1944 movie *Follow the Boys* she sang it to thousands of American troops, just as she actually did many times during the Second World War. She opened every performance of her sold-out season in Las Vegas with the song, and her concerts, including the packed 20,000-seat Hollywood Bowl, always included it. Her last recorded version was made in 1958, just six years before she died.

MacDonald's career was enormously successful with legions of fans and record buyers. Most of her songs were existing compositions. Of those songs composed especially for her to sing in movies, only two – 'San Francisco' and 'Beyond the Blue Horizon' – gained the permanent stamp of her identity. 'Blue Horizon' especially found its own memorable place in history. Jazz greats Peggy Lee and guitarist Les Paul frequently performed it, and it was recorded by talents as diverse as Frankie Laine, pianists Ferrante and Teicher, the Ames Brothers, Johnny Mathis, Artie Shaw, Michael Nesmith and Anita O'Day. It was reported to be a favourite of President John F. Kennedy.

One alteration was made from the original. After the Japanese attack on Pearl Harbor on 7 December 1941, Jeanette MacDonald discreetly changed 'rising sun' to 'shining sun'.

'Won't You Come Home, Bill Bailey' was originally composed for a show called *Town Topics* in 1902. Some people said composer Hugh Cannon wrote the song about a vaudeville performer called Dale B. Dales, whose stage name was Bill Bailey. But in 1973 100-year-old Sarah Bailey Williams told an interviewer that Bill Bailey was the name of her late (first) husband, and he was the original of the song. A frequenter of a bar where Hugh Cannon was pianist, Bailey told him several times that when he stayed late, he got a thunderous reception from the wife back home. Cannon turned this into a song that became a big hit, and exposed the Baileys' home life to comment and ridicule. Sarah Bailey divorced Bill, and claimed 'That darned song broke our marriage'. Bill Bailey died in 1954. Hugh Cannon also wrote another classic standard, 'He Done Me Wrong', later known as 'Frankie and Johnny'.

Ave Maria

Franz Schubert, 1825; J.S. Bach–Charles Gounod, 1859

The Roman Catholic prayer 'Ave Maria' has been set to music dozens of times. The two most recognisable 'Ave Maria' solos in the world are known as the 'Schubert Ave Maria' and the 'Bach-Gounod Ave Maria'. But neither was actually composed as an 'Ave Maria' at all.

The belief persists that Franz Schubert composed the melody to fit the prayer, but this is a complete misconception. His initial contact was with Sir Walter Scott's epic 1810 poem *The Lady of the Lake*, in which a prayer to Maria occurred in a very different guise. Ellen Douglas, the lady, hides with her father in the Scottish Highlands in a cave near Loch Katrine, the lake, to escape the vengeance of the king, who has exiled them. At one point, unhappy and frightened in the cave, Ellen offers a prayer, calling on help from the Virgin Mary. Scott called this offering 'Ellen's Third Song', and it starts with the words 'Ave Maria', but from then on the words depart from the standard prayer and are relevant only in the context of Scott's story.

Ave Maria! maiden mild!
Listen to a maiden's prayer!
Thou canst hear though from the wild,
Thou canst save amid despair.
Safe may we sleep beneath thy care,
Though banish'd, outcast and reviled –
Maiden! hear a maiden's prayer;
Mother, hear a suppliant child!
Ave Maria!
Ave Maria! undefiled!

> The flinty couch we now must share
> Shall seem this down of eider piled,
> If thy protection hover there.
> The murky cavern's heavy air
> Shall breathe of balm if thou hast smiled;
> Then, Maiden! hear a maiden's prayer;
> Mother, list a suppliant child!
> Ave Maria!

It was those words, translated into German by Adam Storck, which appealed to Schubert, and in 1825 he composed his song to fit Scott's words as they sounded in German. The first performance of Schubert's 'Ellens dritter Gesang' (Opus 52 No. 6, D. 839) (Ellen's Third Song) took place in circumstances so obscure that they were not recorded. An unproven legend places it in a castle in the town of Stevregg, to entertain the Countess Weissenwolff who, because of this, became known informally as 'The Lady of the Lake'.

But how did Schubert's melody, originally faithful to Sir Walter Scott's words, morph into a full statement of the Catholic 'Ave Maria' prayer?

The original Schubert composition, with its German version of Scott's words, was first published in 1826. Sometime later (and it is not clear when) someone (and it has never been clear who) managed to fit the Latin words of the 'Ave Maria' prayer to Schubert's melody and the adaptation succeeded well enough to elbow aside Schubert's original intention. But the song known as 'Schubert's Ave Maria' has been recorded over 800 times, and sung in public many hundreds of times more than that.

The Bach-Gounod version could almost be described as the work of a committee. The prayer itself, 'Ave Maria', had variations and additions up to the 15th century but the song we know as the 'Bach-Gounod Ave Maria' has a vocal line composed by one person, an accompaniment composed by someone else – and words fitted to it by yet another person. The generally believed story about its composition is legendary.

The legend is that French composer Charles Gounod was engaged to marry Anna Zimmerman, daughter of Pierre Zimmerman, an official in the Conservatoire National de Musique et de Déclamation in Paris. Zimmerman was a renowned pianist, and teacher to composer Georges Bizet. Gounod was fond of sitting at a piano and improvising, and one evening Zimmerman heard him playing J.S. Bach's Prelude in C major. M. Zimmerman was intrigued that Charles was improvising a pleasant legato melody above the prelude's simple arpeggios. Zimmerman asked if the young man could remember it well enough to play again, which he did, and his future father-in-law sketched out the musical notation.

Within a very short time, Zimmerman had arranged the new combination of Gounod's dreamy improvisation with the Bach prelude, and the combination made its debut performance played on a violin. Zimmerman paid Gounod 200 francs in order to 'own' the work, and sold it to a publisher. In 1852 Gounod married Anna Zimmerman and the following year his melody, supported by an underpinning of Bach, was published as 'Meditation on the 1st Prelude of Bach'.

But by then Gounod had made the acquaintance of a young married woman named Rosalie Jousset, who had a pleasing singing voice. For her, he took his 'Meditation' and added to it some words by the poet Alphonse de Lamartine. These were simultaneously innocent and ambiguous: 'The book of life is the supreme book … one would like to leave open the pages one loves, but the fateful pages turn by themselves'. His intention was to dedicate the new song to Rosalie, but her mother-in-law Aurélie, who was becoming a little fractious about Gounod's attentions, suggested to the composer that the melody seemed to call for a more religious text. So she helped things along by taking the existing song and writing the words of the prayer 'Ave Maria' beneath the existing Lamartine words. The new 'lyrics' did not always fit perfectly, but Gounod was amiable about the idea, and made some minor adjustments to the 'Meditation' tune,

Hail Mary (the prayer)

Hail Mary, full of grace
The Lord is with thee.
Blessed art thou amongst women
And blessed is the fruit of thy womb, Jesus.

Holy Mary, Mother of God
Pray for us, sinners,
Now, and at the hour of our death.
Amen.

and a famous song came into being. Either through an oversight or for a personal religious reason, when Aurélie transcribed the words of the prayer, she omitted the words 'mater Dei' (mother of God).

The song was not published until 1859. By then Gounod had become acquainted with the brilliant virtuoso soprano Madame Miolan-Carvalho, who had created the role of Juliet in his opera *Roméo et Juliette*. He dedicated the new 'Ave Maria' to her and she was first to perform it, on 24 May 1859.

The song became famous across Europe almost immediately. In the minds of the general public, Gounod became indelibly associated with the song, almost eclipsing anything he wrote before or after. There were factions within the Catholic church inclined to cold-shoulder this version, because it omitted 'mater Dei', but a very minor adjustment to the lyrics made room for it to be included (though some singers still stick to Gounod's original). A few classicists didn't approve of Bach having been tinkered with. Camille Saint-Saëns declared Gounod's rearrangement bad taste and called the 'Ave Maria' 'a frog which swelled but did not die, while audiences went delirious in front of the monster'. (Some women actually did faint when the high note was reached.)

But the song's success was unstoppable. Among its many recordings, one of the most unusual could well be the first time it was ever recorded, in 1904. This was a performance by the last known castrato, Alessandro Moreschi, then well over 40. This was not a difficult age for a normal male singer, but castrati, the mega-stars of their era, aged more quickly, and Moreschi was far from his best.

Gilbert and Sullivan's enormously successful *Gondoliers* (1889) drew a sour comment from one critic who complained that the opening phrase of Sullivan's tune 'When a merry maiden marries' bore a worrying resemblance to James Molloy's 'Just a Song at Twilight' (aka 'Love's Old Sweet Song'), which had been published five years before. Unruffled, Sir Arthur Sullivan brushed the comparison aside with the remark, 'Very likely – we only had seven notes between us.'

Both Schubert and Gounod are credited with having 'composed' an 'Ave Maria'. But the curious fact remains that neither of them intended their melody to be transformed into a Catholic prayer. But, after more than a century and a half, anybody who hears either tune says, 'Ave Maria'.

Now is the Hour

When we must say goodbye.

CLEMENT SCOTT, 1913; MAEWA KAIHAU, C.1920

In the era when the piano was king, sheet music of just one song could sell thousands of copies. In 1913, when the Australian firm Palings published a piano solo called 'Swiss Cradle Song', 130,000 copies were sold. One of those found its way to New Zealand and any reference to Switzerland was eliminated when the piano solo was transformed into a Maori song of farewell.

The song had nothing to do with Switzerland anyway. It was composed by a prolific writer of piano solos who lived and worked in Australia, and wrote under the nom-de-plume Clement Scott. Scott was nothing if not internationally minded: his compositions included 'Russian Sleigh Song', 'Belgian Slumber Song', 'Egyptian Love Song', 'German Evening Song', 'Italian Peasant Dance', 'Irish Cradle Song', 'Japanese Lullaby', 'Arabian Night Patrol', 'Flemish Dance', 'Polish Dance' and 'Grecian Legend'.

The 'Swiss Cradle Song' was a pleasant, simple melody, in 4/4 time with a 16-bar theme. It was published with eight variations following the theme, and its cover announced 'violin and cornet parts included gratis'. In spite of impressive sales in its home country of Australia, the song did not leave any lasting mark. But after the music travelled the 2000 kilometres across the Tasman Sea from Australia to New Zealand, it quite quickly gained immortality.

British colonists had come to New Zealand a century earlier, and from them the native Maori people had learned and delighted in the waltz rhythm. Within two years of the 'Swiss Cradle Song' piano solo being published in Australia, Maori in New Zealand had picked up the tune, turned it into 3/4 rhythm and begun developing words for it. One family heard a pianist playing the song to accompany part of a silent movie and liked it, so started fitting Maori words to what they'd heard. Prominent Maori families, the Graces and Awateres, took up the song, passing on words and developing new ones, evolving as they went along what became the Maori song 'Po Ata Rau', with Maori words about dreaming of someone going to a faraway land, and hoping they would return. During the First World War as young men left for the battlefields of Europe, the song was sometimes sung to them.

In 1920 New Zealand was preparing for the visit of the Prince of Wales (later the Duke of Windsor) and Louisa Flavell Kaihau paid attention to the song which had become quite familiar to the Maori people.

Louisa Flavell was descended from both French and Maori aristocracy. The second wife of Henare Kaihau, who was MP for Western Maori from 1896 to 1911, she was known as Maewa Kaihau. An excellent pianist, she was also very attuned to poetry, which she read aloud in an electrifying manner. In honour of the 1920 visit to New Zealand of the Prince of Wales, she set about providing English words for 'Po Ata Rau' and the result was performed to His Royal Highness. After he'd left the country, Maewa Kaihau began announcing that both words and music were her own composition. Palings Publishers didn't agree, and rapidly put one matter straight: they were owners of the tune. There was never total agreement about whether the words of the English version, now called 'Now is the Hour', were entirely Maewa Kaihau's. It was possible that the new lyrics were based on an amalgam of several and various Maori originals.

Maori soprano Ana Hato recorded the song in 1927, and over the following 20 years it became a favourite in New Zealand as the last waltz at dance gatherings, and was de rigueur when passenger ships – and, during wartime, troopships and hospital ships – left the wharf. Bands would play and friends and relatives would sing 'Now is the Hour' as the vessels drew away.

When British star Gracie Fields came to New Zealand on a concert tour in 1945, an amiable Maori driving her between venues taught her 'Now is the Hour'. 'Our Gracie' knew a good song when she heard it, and once back in England she presented it on a popular BBC radio programme, and then recorded it. Gracie Fields made the song known internationally. Her recording was a sensational success, on both sides of the Atlantic; in England it was on the hit parade for 23 weeks. Sales in the United States were so buoyant that a chartered aircraft flew from London carrying a huge number of Gracie's records, and the liner *Queen Mary* was despatched carrying even larger numbers. *Time* magazine described it as 'the biggest shipment of foreign records ever to hit the U.S.'.

Slightly before the song reached the States, one of Bing Crosby's musical advisers in England recommended that he record the song, and he heeded the advice. A maverick writer in New York, Dorothy Stewart, wrote a bridging verse about 'a sunset glow' and the birds 'settling in their nest' and somehow Crosby was persuaded to include this in his performance. So Stewart's name joined the copyright list as one of the lyricists, though the bridge has hardly been sung since.

British star Gracie Fields, who took 'Now is the Hour' out of New Zealand and made it famous worldwide.

But 'Now is the Hour' already had another fairly low-profile American manifestation. In 1936, Irish evangelist Edwin Orr visited New Zealand. After his revival meeting in the small North Island town of Ngaruawahia, he was waiting outside the post office when four young Maori women sang 'Po Ata Rau' to him. Orr, absolutely charmed, scribbled notes about the song and its tune on the back of an envelope. Later, while living in the United States, he reworked the tune into a Christian hymn based on two verses of Psalm 139 and called 'Cleanse me', to what was described, and still is, as 'a Maori melody'. But this could hardly compete with Bing Crosby's version. Released early in 1948, it went onto the American hit parades and stayed at No.1 for three months. It became Crosby's 18th million-seller.

The matter of who composed the tune of 'Now is the Hour' has never been clarified. Clement Scott was said to be a nom-de-plume, either for a man called C.S. Darling or another man called Albert Saunders. In 1948 the manager of the original publisher Palings denied both, saying that Scott was a real person, though nobody else ever seems to have seen him.

The 1927 recording by Ana Hato led a long list of other recording artists. Gracie Fields and Bing Crosby put 'Now is the Hour' into international territory, and those who followed included Kate Smith, the Andrews Sisters, Connie Francis, Marty Robbins, Victor Sylvester, Hank Snow, Burl Ives, Vera Lynn, Kiri Te Kanawa, Pat Boone, Ivan Rebroff and Perry Como.

The theme tune for the 1999 Rugby World Cup, 'World in Union', came from the Jupiter part of Gustav Holst's *Planets Suite*. It had been a hit single for Kiri Te Kanawa before Shirley Bassey and Bryn Terfel sang it at the new rugby stadium in Cardiff.

In 1962 Frank Sinatra arrived in London to make a new recording. Key people in the music and show business world were invited to watch the sessions, and were greatly impressed with the concentrated way in which Sinatra sang his way through the repertoire, which included 'Now is the Hour'. The resulting album was issued under the title *Great Songs of Great Britain*. New Zealanders, who knew better, just acknowledged this as an amusing mistake.

After the Ball

Many a heart is aching, if you could read them all.

CHARLES K. HARRIS, 1892

Charles Kassell Harris was the first songwriter in America to go platinum, selling many millions of sheet-music copies of his songs. There were some who found little to praise, even in his biggest hit, 'After the Ball', but most of the public did not agree.

By the end of the 19th century, popular music had become a booming industry in the United States. The so-called 'Gay Nineties' reverberated to the sound of pianos in parlours, and the selling of sheet music was big business. Harris entered that business in 1885, when he was just 18. He had spent part of his childhood with eight siblings living in a general store where his father also traded in furs. Charles worked as a hotel errand boy and as assistant to a pawnbroker, and grew to have a liking for the music in minstrel shows. Never a man to hide his light under a bushel, young Charles saw a play set around an ice rink, and together with friend Nat Horowitz wrote a song called 'Since Maggie Learned to Skate', which he persuaded the company to include in the play. Then came 'Thou Art Ever in My Thoughts', 'Let's Kiss and Make Up' and 'Creep, Baby, Creep'. The songs were published, and achieved some sales and small royalties, which caused Harris to examine the arithmetic and realise that publishing appeared to bring in more money than writing. Accordingly he established a very small office in Milwaukee with a sign outside saying 'Banjoist and Songwriter – Songs written to order'.

By then Harris had fastened to the belief that successful songs were sad songs. Heartbreak, sorrow, adversity and sentiment were, he believed, what caught attention. This didn't succeed with one of his early offerings, called 'Break the News to Mother', about a fireman killed when trying to stop the destruction of a burning building, at least when the song first appeared.

One night when Harris went out dancing he happened to see a man and woman leave the hall separately, apparently having quarrelled during the evening. Through his mind there floated a line of which he made a note: 'Many a heart is aching, after the ball'. The idea grew, and bloomed into a story about an old man telling a tale to his young niece, who is curious as to why her uncle is alone and unmarried. In 1892 the completed story became the song 'After the Ball'.

The song had a very inauspicious beginning. As author David Ewen tells in *American Popular Songs*, the vaudeville debut of 'After the Ball' was a disaster. The singer, Sam Doctor, forgot the words and the performance was a fiasco. But, only slightly daunted, Harris made a deal with singing star J. Aldrich Libby that, for a discreet 'financial encouragement', he would interpolate the song into Charles Hoyt's hit musical, *A Trip to Chinatown*. This practice was not uncommon in that era. Libby agreed, for $500, and with no warning or explanation, walked onto the stage during Act 2 of *A Trip to Chinatown* and sang 'After the Ball', which had nothing to do with the show's story. At the end of the song there was a stunned silence, then the entire audience arose and applauded for a full five minutes.

From that night on, 'After the Ball' was a market sensation, and became the foundation stone of Charles Harris's publishing, and financial, success. Offered $10,000 in return for the copyright, Harris refused and as the first sheet-music order was for 75,000 copies, he went out and bought another printing press. The song's popularity and success were without equal in their time. Harris became the first composer to have a song whose sheet music sold over one million copies – in fact sheet music sales of 'After the Ball' went over five million, easily surpassing anything published previously. John Philip Sousa included the melody in concerts at the World Exposition in Chicago, to such popular reaction that he retained it in his band's concert repertoire for many years. 'After the Ball' became one of the first American pop hits with a popularity that extended into foreign countries, and the sheet music was translated and published all over Europe.

The song's success eventually caused Charles Harris to make two definite moves. One was physical, from Milwaukee to new offices in the centre of the music publishing business in New York. The second was that the sheet music of every song he composed thereafter, included, under his name, the words 'The composer of "After the Ball"'.

Harris also realised that he could reissue earlier material that hadn't made much of a mark. This meant a new outing for 'Creep, Baby, Creep', which was about an infant being coaxed to crawl. And 'Break the News to Mother', because it resurfaced in 1898 during the Spanish-American War, now concerned a soldier rather than a fireman. This time it was a big hit. It was no wonder that Charles Harris began to be referred to as 'king of the tear-jerkers'.

Unhindered by the fact that he could neither read nor write music, Harris composed and published over 300 more songs. Sometimes they carried a credit saying 'arranged by' which some thought gave scant recognition to his colleagues who actually understood music, and must have put the piano parts together. The public didn't care, and nor did Harris, who continued to make innovations. He was an early advocate of composer promotion and included his own portrait in the design of sheet-music covers, which also included the pictures of the celebrities who sang the songs. This approach was adopted by other publishers as standard practice for decades afterwards. After he'd attended an illustrated lecture about foreign travel, Harris had slides created to illustrate the stories and lyrics of his compositions. The songs were then staged in theatres with not just a singer but also a projector that showed the pictures and the words. A precursor of sub-titles and sur-titles – and, at a pinch, music videos.

Harris also worked towards establishing legal restraints on the use of copyright material and made representations to President Theodore Roosevelt to set this in motion. In 1914 Harris became the inaugural secretary of the American Society of Composers, Authors and Publishers (ASCAP).

Apart from its early interpolation into Charles Hoyt's musical, 'After the Ball' was an 'extra' in another musical 25 years later when, in 1927, Jerome Kern and Oscar Hammerstein chose it to appear in *Show Boat*. Magnolia Ravenal sang 'After the Ball' as she ventured a career as a cabaret entertainer. The song fitted so perfectly into *Show Boat* that it is sometimes forgotten that Kern didn't compose it.

One of Charles Harris's ventures that didn't succeed was his 1910 writing of a screenplay, in the hope of a movie being made around the story of 'After the Ball'. No film company was impressed enough to take on the project. But in later years at least three movies and one theatre musical used the song's title, if not its story.

The first film, in 1924, was a colourful adventure involving a playboy sent to prison by mistake. Another in 1932 starred Vera Ralston, the most famous beauty of her day, known as 'The American Venus', in a frothy story centred on a diplomatic ball in Geneva and bearing a strong resemblance to the Strauss operetta *Die Fledermaus*. *After the Ball* in 1953 was a movie biography of the English male impersonator Vesta

Tilley, and a year later Noel Coward presented *After the Ball*, a musical version of Oscar Wilde's *Lady Windermere's Fan*.

Charles Harris died in 1930, but the title of his most famous song has entered the language. Although formal balls are now far less frequent than they once were, the phrase is used in countless references to matters that have nothing to do with dancing a waltz – a sporting career fading into its twilight, a period of intense activity followed by calm, a burst of publicity starting to dwindle, a political regime whose dominance is fading after a period of power …

'After the Ball' in *Showboat*

Edna Ferber's dramatic novel about America's showboat era was published in 1926 to considerable interest and acclaim. Almost immediately, Jerome Kern and Oscar Hammerstein II began work to transform it into a musical. The story of *Showboat* covers the period from 1870 to the early 1920s. The young heroine Magnolia becomes the leading lady in her family's showboat performances, but is entranced with an itinerant gambler, and against her parents' wishes, leaves the showboat and marries him. Their daughter eventually becomes a Broadway star. By the end of the story in the 1920s, Magnolia is now much older, no longer with her husband, and trying to earn a living as a nightclub singer in less than salubrious surroundings. At this point in the musical, Kern and Hammerstein wanted what in theatre parlance is called a 'prop' song – a song unrelated to the story's action, which simply shows the character singing something. Furthermore, in this case it had to be a song which a nightclub audience would know well enough to join in – which the story required.

The occasional interpolation of songs by other writers was not uncommon at the time, and although it was by then thirty years old, 'After the Ball' was still extremely well known. Interpolation was something Charles Harris understood – it was how he'd launched 'After the Ball'. Arrangements were made between the *Showboat* company and Charles Harris, and Magnolia sang 'After the Ball' in the nightclub scene. It was a perfect choice and has remained in the show ever since. Many people were confused and thought it was actually a composition by Kern and Hammerstein (though they had never for a moment pretended that it was) and some modern references list them as the composers. Not so. And Charles Harris was far too canny about the byways of copyright to have let a false reference influence the payment of percentages for his song into his bank.

After the Ball

A little maiden climbed an old man's knees—
Begged for a story: 'Do uncle, please!
Why are you single, why live alone?
Have you no babies, have you no home?'

'I had a sweetheart, years, years ago,
Where she is now, pet, you will soon know;
List to the story, I'll tell it all:
I believed her faithless after the ball.'

Refrain :
After the ball is over, after the break of morn,
After the dancers' leaving, after the stars are gone,
Many a heart is aching, if you could read them all—
Many the hopes that have vanished after the ball.

'Bright lights were flashing in the grand ballroom,
Softly the music playing sweet tunes.
There came my sweetheart, my love, my own,
"I wish some water; leave me alone."
When I returned, dear, there stood a man
Kissing my sweetheart as lovers can.
Down fell the glass, pet, broken, that's all—
Just as my heart was after the ball.'
Refrain

'Long years have passed, child, I have never wed,
True to my lost love though she is dead.
She tried to tell me, tried to explain—
I would not listen, pleadings were vain.
One day a letter came from that man;
He was her brother, the letter ran.
That's why I'm lonely, no home at all—
I broke her heart, pet, after the ball.'
Refrain

Mad Dogs and Englishmen

Go out in the midday sun.

NOEL COWARD, 1931

Salt and pepper, holly and ivy, Laurel and Hardy, strawberries and cream, bacon and eggs, Jekyll and Hyde – some word pairings are so strong that it is virtually impossible to think of the one without the other. Another that can be added to this list is Noel Coward's coupling of mad dogs with Englishmen. As Frank Sinatra later decreed about love and marriage, they go together like a horse and carriage.

Noel Coward loved to travel, and when still in his early twenties had covered more ground than most of his contemporaries. An early visit to New York and Hollywood, and then Honolulu, ended because of a bout of ill health, and he aimed to set sail again as soon as possible, to more exotic addresses. This happened in late 1929 when Coward and Lord Jeffrey Holmesdale, Earl of Amherst, began a long and complex journey through the East. Coward had mental images of temples by moonlight, vivid jungles and the road to Mandalay complete with flying fish, all seen while travelling first class, of course.

In fact, he and Amherst, with 27 pieces of luggage (including a wind-up gramophone), journeyed by rattling unheated trains, a freight ship carrying copra and salted fish, creaking barges and shaky rental cars. They braved a raging blizzard, avoided an earthquake and at one point found themselves in the middle of a genuine revolution (they ate dinner to the sound of gunfire). At other times they were accompanied by dysentery, mosquitoes, cockroaches, bed-bugs and red soldier ants. Crossing the International Date Line and thus 'losing' a whole day rather dismayed them. They visited Honolulu, Yokohama, Tokyo, Shanghai, Quingdao, Hong Kong, Haiphong, Hanoi, Korea, Saigon, Angkor, Bangkok, Singapore, Kuala Lumpur, Penang and Sri Lanka.

It was, however, a profitable experience. During the trip Coward wrote an entire hit play, *Private Lives*, and a hit song, 'Mad Dogs and Englishmen'. The latter came into being early in 1930 during a week's journey covering the 3200 kilometres between Hanoi and Saigon. The two men travelled by car, surrounded by jungles, rivers, rice paddies and mountains, and en route accidentally demolished stray hens, ducks, dogs, a snake and one cat. Nevertheless, inside Noel Coward's mind there grew an idea from which he started to conceive a complex set of lyrics, and without benefit of pencil or paper, a song took shape. By the time they arrived for a night's stay in a modest guest house surrounded by tropical jungle, the song was complete in Coward's head, and he was able to sing 'Mad Dogs and Englishmen' right through, unaccompanied, to an audience of one – Lord Amherst (though Coward later reported that the tree frogs and lizards gave every indication of approval).

A year later, the song was introduced to the world in New York, sung by Beatrice Lillie in the 1931 revue, *The Third Little Show*, at the Music Box theatre on Broadway. By then Coward was putting together a new revue for London, to be called *Words and Music*. During his visit to Singapore on the long Eastern journey two years before, Coward had seen a young English actor called John Mills, and earmarked him to perform 'Mad Dogs' for the first time in Britain.

This choice caused some dissension with the show's producer, C.B. Cochran, who felt the 24-year-old Mills lacked sufficient maturity or sophistication to put over the song's inherent irony. Curiously, his replacement, to sing this extremely British song, was a Mexican-American known as Romney Brent (his real name was Romulo Larralde). But Brent spoke four languages perfectly, was known for his polished persona and was eight years older than John Mills.

Words and Music opened in 1932, and the lizards and tree frogs who had applauded Coward's first performance of 'Mad Dogs' in a Vietnamese jungle, were proven right. Performed by Romney Brent dressed as a missionary in an unnamed British colony – he wore clerical collar and shorts, and an incongruous leopard-patterned pith helmet, and carried a rolled British umbrella – 'Mad Dogs and Englishmen' became a show-stopper, and has remained so ever since. Noel Coward sang it himself for the following 40 years, and reported rather ruefully that its popularity had somewhat fudged his desire to continue being of Intelligence service to Britain during the Second World War.

Coward had been quietly appropriated by the British government as an agent for

British propaganda in France, and spent several weeks in Paris contacting those about whose movements his superiors were interested in knowing more. But back in London, Coward found that reporting to British authorities by phone required a code language so impenetrable that neither he nor his high-placed British contact could understand a single thing the other was saying.

He decided to aim higher, and having been invited to dinner with Winston Churchill, awaited an opportunity to discuss his possible role as an intelligence officer.

When dinner ended, Noel Coward sat at the piano and sang 'Mad Dogs and Englishmen', then consulted Churchill about what contribution he could make to the war. Churchill puffed his cigar and said, 'Go and sing to them where the guns are firing – that's your job.' So for five years Coward sang to British and American military personnel from Beirut to Burma. He sang about a room with a view, a poor little rich girl, Mrs Worthington's daughter's unsuitability for the stage, the stately homes of England, and, inevitably, 'Mad Dogs and Englishmen'.

Noel Coward sang the first performance of 'Mad Dogs' to frogs and lizards.

Churchill wasn't the only famous fan of the song. When visiting Washington, Noel Coward was invited to dinner with Roosevelt at the White House and, after the meal, entertained at the piano. Roosevelt specifically asked for 'Mad Dogs', and when it was finished, asked for it to be sung again.

On the evening following the signing of the Atlantic Charter in 1941, Churchill hosted Roosevelt at a celebratory dinner on the battleship, HMS *Prince of Wales*. During the evening the two leaders became engaged in debate about the correct sequence of events in 'Mad Dogs and Englishmen'. The debate centred on whether verse one or two ended with the image of people in Bangkok who at twelve o'clock would foam at the mouth and run. Churchill insisted this was the end of verse one but Roosevelt was determined it ended verse two. The matter was somehow checked, and it was discovered that Roosevelt was correct. Churchill took his defeat like a man. Asked later whether the story was true, Churchill admitted that it was.

Although 'Mad Dogs' could be seen as a cruel mockery, it never seemed to upset those it set out to ridicule. Anti-imperialism was far from fashionable in Britain, but Coward's assault on the colonising mentality and the British refusal to adapt to local customs, rose above any political sensitivity because of its tongue-in-cheek impudence and sheer entertainment value.

The song's witty mood and its dazzling collection of brittle imagery and audacious rhymes lifts it from lampoon into light-heartedness. And if for nothing else, Coward's own recorded performances of it in rapid perfect diction have to win praise for their verbal dexterity. He was said to have developed such staccato enunciation with emphatic consonants because his mother was hard of hearing.

Of the 300 songs composed by Noel Coward, 'Mad Dogs and Englishmen' is arguably the most famous. In 1970 the song's fame was unexpectedly highlighted by British rocker Joe Cocker, who chose its title to name his 48-concert tour of the United States. This was followed by recordings of Cocker's four Mad Dogs and Englishmen concerts at Fillmore East, New York, plus other recordings and a film, all later reissued as CDs and DVDs.

Sir David Frost chose Coward's song as one of his BBC *Desert Island Discs* and in 2005 it was sung at the funeral of Mo Mowlam, Britain's former Secretary for Northern Ireland. The rock generation may or may not be able to sing the song but Joe Cocker and many thousands of his fans accepted that the pairing of mad dogs and Englishmen was a permanent part of the English language.

Falling in Love Again

What am I to do? Can't help it.

FRIEDRICH HOLLAENDER, SAMMY LERNER, 1929

It was one of Marlene Dietrich's most famous songs, and featured in almost all her concerts, recordings and television specials. But 'Falling in Love Again' had started out 'vibrating with a nasal sound'.

Its composer Friedrich Hollaender was a classically trained musician who became involved in Berlin's famous cabaret culture during the 1920s. He was a skilful pianist, composer and improviser. At the time, there was a popular musical instrument called a kazoo, defined as 'cigar-shaped and containing a thin diaphragm which vibrates with a nasal sound when the player hums into it'. Initially Hollaender had no interest in the kazoo but in 1929 he attended a circus at which the renowned kazoo player Torello de Balzac performed, and was so impressed with the virtuoso's performance that he immediately composed two pieces for kazoo solo.

In the same year, the famous German actor Emil Jannings visited the equally renowned director Josef von Sternberg, and took him a book. *Professor Unrath*, written by Heinrich Mann and published in 1905, was the story of a teacher who fell in love with a cabaret singer, resigned from his profession and together with her opened a gambling establishment. Von Sternberg was attracted to the idea, and immediately set out to organise a slightly restructured screenplay, a new title, designers, music, filming facilities – and of course an actress to play the cabaret singer.

In later years, director Joseph von Sternberg described his search for the right woman to play the heartless and immoral Lola. Charming and attractive though many of them were, he could not find a young woman who represented what he called *Ewig-Weibliche*, the eternal feminine. Then one night at a local theatre he saw an actress on the stage 'whose face promised everything'. This was Maria Magdalena Sieber, a young German woman who was working in theatre and revues around Berlin, and also, very occasionally, in film. She was asked to audition.

Having discovered that the character of Lola was tarty, Sieber wanted to go to her first audition appointment dressed like a waterfront whore. But her husband Rudolph insisted she dress as a lady. His opinion prevailed and she arrived in a tailored suit, with silver fox furs and white kid gloves. With self-deprecating frankness, she told Josef von Sternberg that she photographed terribly because her nose stuck up like a duck's, and that her hair always looked as if a cat had just licked it. Nevertheless, von Sternberg knew he had found Lola.

Years later he sidestepped the charge that he had 'discovered' the young woman's talent. 'I am a teacher, who took a beautiful woman, instructed her, presented her carefully, edited her charms, disguised her imperfections and led her to crystallise a pictorial aphrodisiac.' And so a legend was born, now called Marlene Dietrich.

The Blue Angel was the first sound movie made in Germany. It was an ambitious project, filmed in German and English, and with music. Friedrich Hollaender was engaged to work on the music for the movie. He was known to, and admired by, the young Dietrich, and her initial reaction to his music was that it was the work of genius, which she enjoyed singing. She was particularly impressed with 'Ich bin die fesche Lola' ('Naughty Lola'), with co-writer Robert Liebmann.

For the second song, Hollaender adapted one of the two kazoo tunes he'd composed some months before, and the result was 'Ich bin von Kopf bis Fuss' ('Falling in Love Again'). But perhaps the transition from kazoo to Dietrich's singing was not so bizarre. Her voice was known less for its beauty than for its husky impact; she was a musical *diseuse*, a teller of stories in semi-song.

On a CD called *Wagner's Rinse Cycle*, a rare 1929 track survives of Torello de Balzac playing the original kazoo solo which became 'Falling in Love Again'.

Delivered in Dietrich's unique style, 'Falling in Love Again' took on an entirely new dimension in everyone's eyes, except Dietrich's. In spite of her usual admiration for Hollaender's work, Dietrich was less than thrilled with this particular song. And because *The Blue Angel* was bilingual, she had to sing the despised song in both languages. Her daughter recalled her describing it as 'something about moths and flames. It's bad enough I have to sing that awful song in English without all the words being changed and now making no sense whatsoever. Thank God once *The Blue Angel* is really finished, I will never have to sing that awful song again.'

Completed at the end of 1929, *The Blue Angel* was released shortly afterwards, and made both Marlene Dietrich and 'Falling in Love Again' famous. Dietrich changed her mind: she sang it for the next 45 years of her career.

Marlene Dietrich in the 1930 movie, The Blue Angel, *which set her on the way to international stardom.*

Happy Birthday

Happy birthday to you, happy birthday dear ....

PATTY AND MILDRED J. HILL, c.1893

The daughters of the Hill family in Kentucky were not the sort of women who put all thoughts of their work behind them at the end of the day. Two of the sisters were teachers. Patty in her own time had developed a set of teaching blocks which became widely used in junior schools throughout the United States. She was also active in the training of junior teachers, and in the 1920s helped to establish the Institute of Child Welfare Research at Columbia University Teachers' College. Her older sister, Mildred, also taught kindergarten, and had an abiding interest in music. She later become a full-time musician and an authority on black American music.

In 1893, when both were teaching at a kindergarten in Louisville, Kentucky, Mildred Hill put together a simple little tune. Whether she composed it entirely out of her head, or was influenced by other 'folk song' fragments, is not clear. But when Patty added seven simple words for lyrics, the groundwork was laid for a very pleasing song. They called it 'Good Morning to All':

> Good morning to you, Good morning to you,
> Good morning, dear children,
> Good morning to all.

'Good Morning to All' was initially intended, and used, as a welcoming song to be sung by the teacher to the class each morning. But when it was published later in 1893, in a book of songs for kindergartens, it proved to be popular in reverse – children sang it to their teachers, rather than the other way round, and the word

153

'children' was popularly replaced by 'teacher'. So the song gently morphed into 'Good Morning to You'.

In this form, young children across the United States began to sing the song, and became familiar with its cadences. The slow development from 'Good Morning' to 'Happy Birthday' seems to have come from children themselves, with encouragement from Patty Hill, who helped to create the new lyric when children liked the song enough to want to sing it at parties away from school.

In 1924 'Good Morning To All', with 'Happy Birthday to You' printed as an optional second verse, was published. By then radio was gaining attention and movies were beginning to take hold. The 'Happy Birthday' words supplanted the earlier version, and in 1931 the song appeared in the Broadway show *Band Wagon*, then became a 'singing telegram' for Western Union in 1933, and surfaced again in Irving Berlin's show *As Thousands Cheer*, in 1934. The third Hill sister, Jessica, believing that Patty and Mildred should have the credit for the now very popular song, and some profit from it, went into battle. Later in 1934 she was able to establish legal copyright to her sisters for their song, and it was officially published in 1935 as 'Happy Birthday'. Since then, two legal changes in the American copyright system have made 'Happy Birthday' copyright until 2030.

Fortunately this does not rule out its being sung privately, as it is at countless parties. It has been named in the *Guinness Book of Records* as one of the three most-sung songs in the English language, along with 'For He's a Jolly Good Fellow' and 'Auld Lang Syne'. But the copyright can be enforced when the song is used in a public place where a larger group than a family is gathered, such as a sports event. Royalties must be paid if the song is ever part of a profit-making enterprise, such as being included in a television show, a commercial stage performance or movie; or being built into toys, music boxes, watches, mobile phones and 'singing' birthday cards.

The copyright sometimes shows its teeth. Leonard Bernstein's 1944 musical *On the Town* featured a fragment of 'Happy Birthday' in a nightclub scene. Soon after its opening, the show was threatened by the song's owners, permission to use it was withheld and the fragment disappeared from the score. American classical composer Roy Harris's symphonic piece 'Celebration' was a tribute to fellow composer Howard Hanson, and included references to the 'Happy Birthday' tune. After 'Celebration's premiere by the Boston Symphony Orchestra in 1946, the show-business magazine *Variety* reported that Harris, having been notified of the copyright law, had been obliged to remove the offending section. Even esteemed Russian composer Igor Stravinsky fell foul of the legal system. Having heard orchestral members sing and play 'Happy Birthday', in 1955 he used the melody in a symphonic composition, assuming it was a folk song. He was firmly told it was not.

In order to deal with their fully copyrighted property, the Hill sisters established a foundation through which royalties were paid until their death, and which still receives several million dollars of income a year. In 2002 the mayor of Louisville dedicated a Happy Birthday parking lot near Main Street, with a commemorative plaque telling the story of the local sisters who composed the famous song.

Although 'Happy Birthday' has only four short musical phrases, and a single repetitive line of words, it has become a familiar part of the musical landscape. It is sung all over the world in many languages – by one estimate several million times a year – often to children who are too young even to know what the song is about, but also to just about everyone else. Two performances of the song are particularly famous. At President John F. Kennedy's birthday concert in May 1962, Marilyn Monroe gave a brief but sultry and memorable performance of the song. Sadly, it was Monroe's last major public appearance; she died three months later. Seven years afterwards, in 1969, the song had its longest-distance broadcast when the crew of the orbiting Apollo 9 sang 'Happy Birthday' to NASA director Christopher Kraft.

A memorable performance. Marilyn Monroe sings 'Happy Birthday' to President John Kennedy, May 1962.

Candle in the Wind

Though I never knew you at all.

ELTON JOHN, BERNIE TAUPIN, 1973

When he was 11, Reginald Dwight won a scholarship to the Royal Academy of Music to learn formal classical music: theory, harmony, structure and composition. But when he discovered Elvis Presley, Dwight's tastes were no longer inclined to be classical. He was 15 when Marilyn Monroe died. Eleven years later he immortalised her iconic image in song, and then in 1997 he did it all over again for another icon.

Reg Dwight wasn't an entirely devoted student. His ear was so good that he could sit at the keyboard and play a Handel piano solo he'd heard only once. Besides liking Handel and Bach, he also had a taste for performing, and sang in the academy choir. But he was already creating music of his own, in between music training, standard schooling and part-time jobs delivering newspapers and working in a wine shop.

Having served an apprenticeship as a pianist in a suburban pub, where he had to play a wide range of repertoire to please the sometimes rowdy locals, the young musician eventually formed a band, which reached the status of backing more prominent singers and musicians and was a support act for blues legend Long John Baldry.

Then one day Dwight answered a job advertisement from a music publishing firm and told one of its managers of his interest in writing music. Another young man who had answered the same advertisement had written some lyrics, but without music. The lyrics were handed to Reg Dwight, who had decided to change his name. In honour of two British musicians, jazz saxophonist Elton Dean and John Baldry, he legally became Elton John.

He composed tunes to fit the lyrics he'd been handed, and posted the combination to the other young applicant, Bernie Taupin. In 1967 their first song, 'I'm Going Home', was recorded by Simon Dupree, but not released until 2004. And so began one of the great musical partnerships.

Success wasn't immediate. Their first album two years later caused no waves, and they embarked on a period of writing music for other artists to perform. In 1970, however, their own piece, 'Your Song', went into the American Top 10, and the album from which it came, *Border Song*, followed soon after. Elton John's concert at the Troubadour in Los Angeles was a sensational success, and his American status was established from that point.

In the following years, Elton John's musical output and successes, both artistic and financial, rose to dizzying heights. Hits like 'Rocket Man', 'Friends', 'Honky Cat' and 'Crocodile Rock' came from albums that were rapidly advancing his name and fame. In 1973, a double album called *Goodbye Yellow Brick Road* became an immediate success, and topped charts in both Britain and the United States.

The album's title song concerned a young man who had hoped that in finding the legendary Emerald City, his troubles and problems would disappear, to be replaced by optimism and opportunities. But having arrived, he is disappointed by the city's exploitive values and decides to return home – on the yellow brick road. Although it is not mentioned directly, the imagery in the lyrics has fairly distinct echoes of *The Wizard of Oz*, and also of Judy Garland herself, who had died four years before the song was written.

Another song on the same album, 'Goodbye Norma Jean', was a direct reference to another movie star. During the 1950s Marilyn Monroe, born Norma Jeane Mortenson, was one of the most famous women in the world. She effortlessly conveyed a combination of acute vulnerability and bold sexiness which audiences found irresistible. Men found her the epitome of attraction, and women seemed unthreatened by her helplessness. Although rather like a puppy version of Mae West, she was certainly no mere kewpie doll. Her improbable voice and fine instinct for timing, combined with an appeal that can only be described as magic, made her a mega-star. Sir Laurence Olivier said of her that in the short space between the lens and the celluloid itself a miracle took place. Although not usually thought of as a musical performer, she sang in five of the 29 movies in which she appeared, albeit with a little help from famous voice-dubber Marni Nixon with the high notes in her most famous number, 'Diamonds are a Girl's Best Friend' from *Gentlemen Prefer Blondes*.

Marilyn's death in 1962 at the age of 36 created shock waves throughout the world. The exact circumstances leading to her death have never been satisfactorily clarified. Even after her death, the interest scarcely died. More than 500 books have been written about her. Almost a decade after Marilyn Monroe's death, lyricist Bernie Taupin noticed the phrase 'candle in the wind' in a newspaper account of the death of rock star Janis Joplin in 1970. When he started work on the new song, it could have focused on Joplin, movie star James Dean or singer Jim Morrison, all of whom died young. But it was Marilyn Monroe, in the person of Norma Jean, who became the subject of 'Candle in the Wind'.

After the album *Goodbye Yellow Brick Road* was released in 1973, the 'Marilyn' song was well received, and reached a chart position in 1974, but then faded somewhat, eclipsed by other Elton John–Bernie Taupin successes. Elton John's flamboyant fashion sense and distinctive piano style were causing his concert appearances to become major events, but by 1987 he developed nodules on his vocal chords, giving his voice an unaccustomed grittiness. Before the operation to remedy this, he recorded a live concert with the Melbourne Symphony Orchestra, which featured a fresh performance of 'Candle in the Wind'. This recording was extremely well received, and in 1988 the song found a new, greater popularity. Although it definitely fitted into the context of rock, its slow, anthem-like solemnity created a touching sincerity.

By the time the Melbourne recording was released, the former Lady Diana Spencer had been Princess of Wales for seven years. Hers was not an ugly-duckling-into-swan situation – she was young and beautiful before her marriage to Prince Charles – but what surprised everyone was her amazing transformation from shy kindergarten teacher into blazing celebrity status. Her every move, every day, was front-page news, at first in Britain and then worldwide. The royal family had never had anyone like this.

And though the Queen's sister, Princess Margaret, had friendships with celebrities like Danny Kaye and Peter Sellers, Diana made no bones about her liking for a greater range of company well outside the usual royal and diplomatic circles. She was comfortable with entertainment figures, and they with her. Some referred to her circle of friends as an alternative show-biz court, which included Tom Hanks, Luciano Pavarotti, Michael Barrymore, Sting, George Michael and Elton John.

Diana and Elton John had met in 1981 before her wedding to Prince Charles. The rock star had been engaged to play at a birthday party for Charles's brother, Prince Andrew and afterwards had joined the party. Diana asked him to dance the Charleston with her. John later confessed that he'd never Charlestoned before but couldn't turn down an about-to-be princess. From that night, their friendship grew – telephone calls, parties, dinners, lunches, the occasional falling out, then more telephone calls, dinners and so on. Elton told American television interviewer Barbara Walters that during a party at his own house, Princess Diana was intrigued to find Richard Gere there and spent almost all evening sitting on the floor talking to him. With Elton John, the princess was prepared to acknowledge the pressure she felt from ceaseless publicity, knowing that he was in a not dissimilar position. Both knew that the goldfish bowl life was far from easy, and John was aware that, amid the glamour of her life, she felt occasional desolation about the almost painful scrutiny to which her every move was subjected.

When Gianni Versace died, Elton flew to the funeral and was relieved to see Diana there. She asked if she could sit next to him and embraced him comfortingly. No one could have known that Diana herself had only one more month to live.

In August 1997 the death of Diana, Princess of Wales shocked the world. The tributes were neverending, to her beauty and vivacity, her use of her profile to raise vast sums for charities, her boldness in changing public perceptions of serious matters like Aids and land mines, her fresh approach to public behaviour and her wholesome relationship with her children. And as comment and interviews proliferated on television, someone in a broadcasting newsroom had the idea of playing Elton John's recording of 'Candle in the Wind' behind photo montages of the late princess.

Diana's elder sister Lady Sarah McCorquodale phoned Elton John and asked if he would sing at Diana's funeral. He was willing, but the suggestion had to go through a maze of permissions involving the royal family and Westminster Abbey's administration, before the matter was settled. By then, the public had become accustomed to the association of 'Candle in the Wind' with images of the beautiful young smiling princess. And, like Marilyn Monroe, she was a major international icon, whose life had been devastatingly cut short, at the same age of 36.

Elton John, however, had the sense – and the class – to realise that in spite of the links between the two women, it would be quite inappropriate to sing the song with its original lyrics. But there was very little time to create Diana-centred lyrics. Bernie Taupin, also sincerely upset by Diana's death, set to with fierce concentration and composed a new set of words in less than two hours.

Over a million people lined the streets of London on the day of the Princess of Wales's funeral, and the live telecast was watched by an estimated 2.5 billion – some said it was half the known population of the world. A prominent part of the service was Elton John, alone at a grand piano, giving an emotional performance of the new version of 'Candle in the Wind', now called 'Goodbye English Rose'. Only hours after the service ended, he went into a recording studio and sang the song for a second time, now with the addition of a string quartet and woodwinds. Then he announced that he would never sing the tribute again.

Westminster Abbey, 6 September 1997. Sir Elton John sings his tribute to Diana, Princess of Wales, during her funeral.

The recording, released a few days later, sold 658,000 copies the first day, and a further 1.5 million within its first week, holding the position of top single for five weeks. In the United States, it also sold over a million in its first week, went straight to the top and stayed there for 14 weeks. Eventually the combined record sales worldwide were over 33 million copies.

In February 1998, Taupin's original handwritten lyrics for the Diana version of 'Candle in the Wind' were put up for auction. Signed and authenticated by both Taupin and Elton John, the four sheets of paper included three working stages, complete with crossings-out and revisions, and the final typed sheet as faxed to John by Taupin from California. The BBC reported that bidding was brisk, and an American businessman won, paying $442,500. The money was to be handed over to the Children's Hospital in Los Angeles, on behalf of the Princess of Wales Memorial Fund. All the profits from the 'Goodbye English Rose' recording were donated to the fund and, in spite of constant requests, Elton John has declined to sing it. All concert performances of 'Candle in the Wind' since have been the 1973 version.

During Diana's funeral, her brother Lord Charles Spencer commented on the irony that although his sister's name was that of the ancient Greek goddess of hunting, she had herself become the most hunted woman in the world. Hunted she was, but Sir Elton John has certainly contributed to her not being forgotten.

When you walk through a storm, hold your head up high.
It is a fact, and not a put-down, that the name of Christine Johnson is not known to the wider world. But she introduced the world to a song that has now been sung by thousands of people at certain kinds of sports matches. A Metropolitan Opera mezzo, Johnson played Cousin Nettie in the first-ever production of Rodgers and Hammerstein's musical, *Carousel*, in New York in April 1945. Thus she was the first person to sing 'You'll Never Walk Alone'. Another Met star, Claramae Turner, provided a lustrous version in the 1956 movie. Some time after, the song became a leitmotif for American graduation ceremonies, and also several decades of British football matches.

A Manchester amateur operatic society claims it was rehearsing *Carousel* in 1958 when a tragic air crash in Germany killed eight well-known Manchester football players. As a tribute, the operatic group sang the musical's hit song at the next football match at Old Trafford sports ground. The supporters of Manchester United's football team rapidly took up the same song and sang it at every match following. Supporters of Liverpool football appear to have taken up the same song some five years later, and like Manchester, it assumed an anthem quality for team matches there. Either way, there can't be many Broadway show tunes that are frequently sung in full-throated unison by crowds of up to 80,000.

Waltzing Matilda

Once a jolly swagman camped by a billabong.

CHRISTINA MACPHERSON, BANJO PATERSON, 1903

In April 1894 Miss Christina Macpherson went to the annual race meeting in Warrnambool, on the south coast of Australia. She had a good ear for music, and one of the Scottish tunes played by the band on the lawn near the course appealed to her. So when she went home she sat at the piano and played it as best she could remember. It eventually became Australia's favourite song.

The melody she liked was based on a Scottish song called 'Thou Bonny Wood of Craigielee', thought to date back to the early years of the 19th century. Warrnambool's Garrison Artillery Band had played the instrumental version, billed just as 'Craigielee'.

Eight months later, Christina Macpherson, her father and sister travelled north to visit Christina's brothers on their sheep-rearing property in Dagworth. En route, the group broke their days-long journey in the settlement of Winton, where Christina Macpherson met up with an old school friend, Sarah Riley, who was now engaged to a young solicitor. Sarah was invited to travel north and spend Christmas with the Macphersons, and to bring her fiancé, Andrew Paterson, with her.

Paterson was not just a lawyer. Since 1885 the Sydney edition of *The Bulletin* had been publishing his poetry, under the pseudonym of 'The Banjo', after his favourite horse. In 1890 he had written 'The Man from Snowy River' and earlier in 1895 his first book of 'bush ballads' had been published under that name.

It was a merry group of family and friends who gathered on the Dagworth property that December of 1894. Paterson loved the outdoors and horse riding, so the local legend tells that he was taken out riding one day by Christina's brother, Robert. They visited a pool known as the Scour Hole, where wool was washed. There they stopped and Robert Macpherson pointed out the unusual sight of a solitary grave, identified only by a simple post. It marked the burial place of a wool-scourer called George Pope who had drowned in the Scour Hole in 1891. His was the only drowning recorded in the district up to that date.

Although the Dagworth sheep station had no piano, there was an old auto-harp, or zither. On this, even though she had never played one before, Christina Macpherson did her best to provide music. And one tune she played many times was her favourite 'Craigielee', possibly a bit blurred from the time she'd heard it months before, and now being played on an inadequate instrument. But Banjo Paterson liked it too. He asked if there were any words but was told there were none.

Then one night he heard a fellow guest remark that he'd seen a swagman 'waltzing Matilda'. Locals explained that this expression referred to an itinerant worker carrying a bundle of absolutely basic necessities – a swag – as he tramped from place to place. This was sometimes known as 'humping the drum', but in that part of Australia, because his bundle swayed with him as he walked along, and was the only dancing partner he would be likely to see for months on end, carrying a swag was called 'waltzing Matilda'.

Banjo Paterson clearly felt a synergy between the expression he'd just learned and the attractive tune played by Christina Macpherson at Dagworth. Gradually a poem emerged from Banjo. After he and Sarah Riley (whom he did not actually marry) had left, the family and guests remaining at Dagworth sang this song frequently and its popularity soon spread to neighbouring districts. Less than a year after Christina Macpherson had heard 'Craigielee', its newborn descendant 'Waltzing Matilda' was sung by cheerful locals in Winton at a formal banquet held for the Premier of the State of Queensland, Hugh Nelson. But publication was still many years away.

The song spread quite quickly into further rural areas. Sheep farmers and sheep shearers sang it. Cooks sang it in sheep-station kitchens, drovers sang it around camp fires and swagmen sang it through the bushlands. As always happens with itinerant songs, small alterations in tune and words crept in along the way. Eventually Christina Macpherson wrote out her version of the tune, with Banjo Paterson's words added, and gave it to a stock and station agent she knew, W. B. Bartlam. During the late decades of the 1800s Bartlam managed Marathon station, which adjoined Dagworth. Bartlam's family were frequent guests at Dagworth and heard the song about Matilda waltzing. Christina Macpherson's handwritten music-and-words of the Matilda song was inherited by the Bartlam family, and remained in obscurity until 1971.

Love Me Tender

In 1969 Scotsman Eric Bogle emigrated to Australia, where he watched Australians on Anzac Day, 25 April, commemorating soldiers who had died in the First World War and later conflicts. Moved by the ceremony, Bogle composed a haunting ballad about young Australian men travelling to a distant battle. Pulling no punches about the devastation of wars and the misery of men who fight them, the song incorporated part of the melody and lyrics of the original 'Waltzing Matilda', which is referred to as the song a band is playing as the troopship leaves home. Bogle called the song 'The Band Played Waltzing Matilda'.

Some time after he'd written it, Bogle was competing in a folksinging contest. As his second-choice item he sang 'The Band Played Waltzing Matilda' and won third prize. The song filtered to Britain more or less by accident in 1974. Jane Herivel had listened to Bogle, liked what she heard, and sang it in England. British folk star June Tabor heard Herivel, and also liked the song, so recorded it. Her version engendered considerable popularity for the song in Britain and Ireland, and hers was the first of over 100 other recordings – in English, Portuguese, Danish and Spanish – by The Pogues, Joan Baez, The Clancy Brothers, Slim Dusty, The Dubliners and John McDermott, to name but a few.

Even to people unfamiliar with the iconic status in Australia of the original 'Waltzing Matilda', Bogle's song achieved respect internationally among a generation that regarded it as a passionate anti-war statement. Bogle's lyrics refused to glorify war, but instead drew attention to the painful and unnecessary loss of life and dignity it caused. Although it is distinctly Australian, and speaks of the far-distant military tragedies of the Dardanelles in 1915, 'The Band Played Waltzing Matilda' has a message that is seen as timeless.

When Australian men, many of them from rural districts, left after 1899 to fight in the South African War, 'Waltzing Matilda' became popular among soldiers, and also started to be heard in Sydney. The song mentioned the swagman watching and waiting for his billy to boil so he could make a cup of tea. (A billy is an abbreviation of 'billycan', a tin vessel commonly used for boiling water over a fire.) James Inglis, a Sydney importer of tea, noticed this reference and wondered how he could use 'Waltzing Matilda' to advertise his product, the judiciously branded Billy Tea, which featured, on the packet, a bushman with a billy, a mug of tea and a kangaroo. He began to make enquiries about who to approach about using the song as an advertising stunt or 'singing commercial'.

Communications weren't easy in that huge country, and it has never been clear how Inglis secured 'permission' to publish the song. He asked Marie Cowan, the wife of his firm's manager, to 'arrange' the tune and give it a piano accompaniment, and some discreet alterations were made in the words, mainly to highlight the swagman's billy and the tea. Although the song was published in 1903 with a clear announcement 'Music arranged by Marie Cowan', public vagueness about what 'arranged' meant gave rise to a belief that Marie Cowan had composed the tune. But this version at least focused all the disparate variations of words and tune that had been circulating for years into the 'Waltzing Matilda' we know today.

Marie Cowan died in 1919, and soon afterwards the music publishing company, Allan's, bought the rights to her 'arrangement' and continued to promote her as 'composer', until the Christina Macpherson story began to emerge. The acquisition by Allan's also brought to an end the song's relationship with the tea company.

'Waltzing Matilda' appeared in a students' songbook in 1911, then in a songbook for Australian soldiers. Where the Australian diggers went during the First World War, Matilda went too. Later, she surfaced in England in a publication called *Poetry for the People*. And thousands of American troops stationed in Australia during the Second World War liked the song and took it home with them – Matilda became a war bride in the USA. Back home in Australia 'Waltzing Matilda' was sung to welcome Queen Elizabeth when she arrived for a royal tour in 1954, and by the time Australia hosted the Olympic Games in 1956, the song was heard in the closing ceremony, performed by massed choirs. It was clear by then that the whole of Australia knew and loved Matilda.

Her fame became international when the 1959 movie *On the Beach* was released. Based on the novel by Nevil Shute, its story concerned the world at nuclear war, with Australia as the last safe place. The 'Waltzing Matilda' theme occurred throughout the movie in various contexts, from drunken fishermen to a romantic background for Gregory Peck and Ava Gardner. The movie was a great success and brought Matilda a wider audience.

Allan's negotiated the publishing of 'Waltzing Matilda' in over 30 countries and because of a requirement made by arranger Marie Cowan's widower at the time Allan's acquired the rights, part of all profits went to charities in Australia. Matilda probably reached her biggest instant audience at the Sydney 2000 Olympics closing ceremony when, in a worldwide telecast, Australian country music icon Slim Dusty sang the song and a stadium of 110,000 people joined in.

The slight eccentricity of the song attracted accomplished recording artists who were slightly outside the musical mainstream: Rolf Harris, Burl Ives, Chubby Checker, the Irish Rovers, the Coldstream Guards and the Red Army Choir. There were also some Matilda-inspired offerings from Harry Belafonte, Bill Haley, Eric Bogle, The Pogues and Tom Waits. One truly unusual recording featured 'Waltzing Matilda' played by a band of bagpipes.

The possibility that 'Waltzing Matilda' could or should become Australia's officially recognised national anthem, perhaps at least the official national song, has surfaced many times, but without resolution. There is no doubt that the entire population of Australia knows the song better than they know their real anthem, 'Advance, Australia Fair', but the naysayers point out that it makes no reference to national pride, confidence or history; that it doesn't stand for anything; it is just a folk ballad telling a sad tale with an illogically optimistic melody. Can a song about a tramp of doubtful integrity, who commits suicide because of a stolen sheep, be taken seriously?

Those supporting a possible national status for the song reply that it is a symbol of Australian nationality, which is slightly different from being a symbol of nationhood. There have even been attempts to set new, more 'national' words to the tune. But the powers that be hold firm: much as it is loved there, 'Waltzing Matilda' holds no official status in Australia.

Copyrights on 'Waltzing Matilda' expired in Australia in 1991, but not in the United States. Because of the long-distant misinterpretation of Marie Cowan's role, a problem was found when it emerged that Allan's had licensed an American copyright (as of 1941 held by Carl Fischer Inc.) with her identified as the composer. Thus, after various renewals, the commonly accepted tune remains under copyright in the States until 2011 and any performance of the song there must be paid for. At the Atlanta Olympics in 1996, Australia had to pay to use its own song.

Although this situation causes shock and horror back in Australia, it does not for one moment dent Australians' identification with and loyalty to the Paterson/Macpherson song. The Australian women's national soccer team is called The Matildas. At the Warrnambool Racecourse where Christina Macpherson first heard the band play 'Craigielee', there is now a Matilda Room with a prime view of the course, and of the lawn where she heard the band play. And the song's final quirk, which only adds to its charm, is that in spite of the title and the chorus, 'Waltzing Matilda' isn't actually a waltz.

Send in the Clowns

Isn't it rich?

STEPHEN SONDHEIM, 1973

American composer Stephen Sondheim had 15 years of successful musicals behind him before he turned his attention to Ingmar Bergman's 1955 film, *Smiles of a Summer Night*. Bergman was one of the most famous directors in the world, but his films tended to be dark, intense and soul-searching. *Smiles of a Summer Night* was different – light, amusing and charming. Paradoxically, it was conceived during a difficult period in his personal life. In the early 1950s his marriage had ended, replaced by a relationship fraught with its own problems. His previous films were not bringing financial security either to him or the distributors, and he was dogged by pain. Nevertheless, arising from these sombre shadows came one of the most delightful movies of the decade, which itself later gave rise to an elegant musical and a haunting song.

The film's plot told of a young man in love with his stepmother, who is equally young and, though married to his father, still a virgin. Around those two there whirled six other characters, each in some way involved with one of the others. The weaving in and out of relationships – actual, desired or merely observed – created a farce-like story that was simultaneously elegant, funny and sad.

Bergman's title seemed to owe a nod to Shakespeare's *A Midsummer Night's Dream* but the two plays differed in many aspects. Each involved its characters in complex and amusing intrigues, Bergman's more in line with the traditions of French farce. The smiles of his title were a fanciful reference to the slow descent of evening into darkness, during which the night 'smiled' first at the young who knew nothing, second at the fools who knew too little and third at the old, who knew too much. Central to all the action is the character of Desiree Armfeldt, a famous actress who has a love child by a former lover – who is now married to a younger woman. His own son (by a former marriage) lusts after his new stepmother, and tries to refocus his lust on the household maid … and emotional complications arose between everyone concerned.

In his early years, Sondheim had attempted to set the original *Mary Poppins* stories as a theatre musical, but was stymied by the holders of the Poppins copyright who would not grant him the production rights. Later the rights famously went to the Disney organisation, with music by the Sherman brothers, resulting in an Oscar, a Grammy, stardom for Julie Andrews and eventually a stage musical in 2004. Sondheim had also, in 1956, cast his eye on Jean Anouilh's play *Ring Around the Moon* but again was told no. But in the same year, when *Smiles of a Summer Night* won a special prize at the Cannes Film Festival, Sondheim was asked to write the lyrics for a new show to be called *West Side Story*, which established him as a major artist in the American musical theatre. After that he had great success as either lyricist or composer for *Gypsy*, *A Funny Thing Happened on the Way to the Forum*, *Do I Hear a Waltz?*, *Company* and *Follies* – a glittering list.

During those years, Sondheim had nurtured an idea of writing a work entirely in waltz rhythms. After *Follies*, in 1971, Sondheim began to study Bergman's movie *Smiles of a Summer Night* – and gradually a musical began to form. Ingmar Bergman's work seldom ventured into music, but he knew about waltzes. His writings reveal that he could remember, even aged five, sitting under the table imagining the pictures on the wall to be 'moving', while from the next door apartment came the music of a piano playing waltzes – only waltzes. Either through his own research into Bergman's life, or by sheer coincidence, Sondheim composed a musical which was waltzes – only waltzes. The show's title was taken directly from Mozart's instrumental serenade, 'Eine Kleine Nachtmusik' (1787). And the Bergman plot, in Hugh Wheeler's adaptation with Sondheim's music, became more than reminiscent of a Mozartian romp, with characters in period costumes involved in a romantic advance-and-retreat among beautiful surroundings, to refined and graceful music.

Treading ground covered over a decade before, when *My Fair Lady* had triumphed with a leading man who couldn't really sing, Sondheim aimed for a cast of actors-who-could sing, rather that singers-who-might-be-able-to-act. At the time, British star Glynis Johns seemed a strange choice to play the famous actress Desiree Armfeldt. A delightful and winning performer, she had been a memorable mermaid in *Miranda*, Maid Jean to Danny Kaye's *Court Jester*, Lady Penelope Peasoup in *Batman*, and Julie

Andrews' employer in *Mary Poppins* – in which 'Sister Suffragette' was the only piece of singing anyone could remember her doing. Playing opposite her, leading man Len Cariou had a magnificent voice, besides being a Theatre World Award-winning actor. And completing the star trio was the formidable character comedienne, Hermione Gingold.

The musical was still progressing through its creative stages when it was discovered that, for balance, one scene seemed to need a new song for the leading man, so Sondheim went home to work on it. Three days later he came in and called people around the piano. Cariou was eagerly awaiting 'his' new song when Sondheim said to him, regretfully, that the song had turned out to be for Glynis Johns. And he played 'Send in the Clowns'. Once he'd heard Johns sing the song, Cariou remained adamant that nobody else's performance could better hers.

A Little Night Music opened in February 1973, to impressive acclaim, and was described as an adult musical. Even though slightly out of line with what is usually considered a Broadway show, this operetta-style work with its all-three-quarter-time waltz score was a triumph. And one of its most successful moments was Glynis Johns singing 'Send in the Clowns'.

Sondheim had especially tailored the song to his star's minimal singing voice – simple brief phrases, clipped words, almost nothing sustained, plenty of places to breathe. The song's deliberately fragile and fragmented melody never gave the audience an impression that its statement-like quality was a fault of the singer's

British star Glynis Johns, for whom 'Send in the Clowns' was composed.

performance. For Glynis Johns it was perfect. Her singing tone was described by one observer as being the cousin of bullfrogs, and by another, more kindly, as 'silver'. But the combination she achieved, of repressed anger and desperate regret, had audiences in the palm of her hand. She was not a classic beauty – her features had been called 'bruised' and her smile 'blurry', and Walter Kerr said she had the air of 'a consort of weary gods' – but as Desiree Armfeldt she was ideal. As Arthur Jackson wrote in *The Book of Musicals*, 'Her odd little non-singing voice added the true heart-break quality called for in the context of the story.'

A Little Night Music was a hit show and, night after night, Glynis Johns' performance of 'Send in the Clowns' was the hit of the hit. The show earned the Drama Critics' award as Best Musical of the Year, and five Tony Awards, including Best Musical, Sondheim for Best Score and Glynis Johns for Best Actress in a Musical.

Later Desirees were Jean Simmons and then Dame Judi Dench. Neither was a 'real' singer, though Dench had bawled her way through the role of Sally Bowles in the London production of *Cabaret* to great acclaim. As Desiree she was a huge success, blending devastating comedy with such vulnerability that the *Daily Telegraph* decreed she made 'Send in the Clowns' almost unbearably moving.

The structure of Sondheim's lyrics and music often made his songs so integral to the action that they didn't really have a life as off-stage solo items. But 'Send in the Clowns' could and did stand alone and has been recorded by a stellar list: Judy Collins, Cleo Laine, Frank Sinatra, Shirley Bassey, Van Morrison, Bryn Terfel and Barbra Streisand (for whom Sondheim wrote extra new lyrics). It has been performed in concert by Julie Andrews, Glenn Close and even Krusty the clown, during a *Simpsons* insert to a Sondheim birthday gala at the Hollywood Bowl in 2005.

Almost as unlikely as Krusty the Clown's was the performance of 'Send in the Clowns' by Elizabeth Taylor. Work started on the film version of *A Little Night Music* in 1976. It was intended as a vehicle for Taylor who, at 45, was exactly the right age for Desiree Armfeldt and was as famous in real life as her character was in the story. But when the film came out in March 1978 on limited release, it gathered mainly discouraging reviews. Harold Prince's direction was decreed unsuitable for a delicate musical, and *Newsweek* said of Elizabeth Taylor that 'the audience is likely to respond to her overblown presence as if she were a character out of Al Capp'. *Cue* magazine described her as 'all calories, cleavage and camp'.

There was much speculation about her singing. Elizabeth Taylor had seemed to sing in three previous movies – aged 10 in *There's One Born Every Minute* (1942), in *Cynthia* (1947) and in *A Date with Judy* (1948) – but these were believed to have been dubbed. This time, it had been announced that she would actually sing. But when the movie was released there was dispute. Did Elaine Tomkinson dub for her? Taylor's biographer Andrew Budgell said it was the actress's own voice and he was backed up incontrovertibly by Len Cariou, who was present at the recording session.

Cariou told Craig Zadan, author of *Sondheim and Co.*, that he had arrived at the recording session to find Elizabeth Taylor sitting with a full symphony orchestra waiting to sing 'Send in the Clowns'. She 'seemed scared' and was having trouble starting to sing on the right beat at the right moment. An experienced singer himself, Cariou sat with her, one hand on her shoulder, and with gentle pressing and pointing at appropriate moments, guided her through the session. Later, in an interview with the *San Diego Union*, Taylor agreed with Cariou's description and admitted that she was 'petrified'. '"Send in the Clowns" is one of my favourite songs, but everyone in the world has recorded it and here comes dumbbell to sing it. They put me in a little glass box with earphones on and I felt like a prisoner of war – it was me against the world.' But Elizabeth Taylor's appealing self-deprecation didn't save the movie. One critic said her singing made Glynis Johns seem like Lily Pons. Others found her singing no better or worse that other 'non-singers' who had played the role but felt that she couldn't convey the heart-breaking vulnerability achieved by Glynis Johns.

The seldom-mentioned movie of *A Little Night Music* did nothing to dent the popularity of 'Send in the Clowns'. Besides its highly individual style, haunting lyrics and simple pace, the song has one very unusual feature: unlike many popular hits, it is not intended to be sung by the young in love, but by a mature performer who has seen it all before. The song remains an anthem to regret for unwise decisions in the past and recognition that there's no need to send in the clowns – they're already here.

Greensleeves

Greensleeves was all my joy, Greensleeves was my delight.

Anon., 1584

Did King Henry VIII compose it? Many people believe so. But it was not published until over 30 years after the old lecher had died, and without any reference to its composer, noble or otherwise.

In Europe, music began to be printed and sold during the 15th century, when an early form of 'licence to print' existed. But it was impossible to control melodies being sung in many different places, in troubadour style, and gathering widely varying words as they went. In general, a good melody is harder to create than good words, so when an attractive tune became available, from whatever source, it was seized upon and different words were added for various locations and occasions. The melody itself would also undergo subtle changes.

There is no doubt that King Henry was a star, and a good musician when he was young. The Venetian ambassador Piero Pasqualigo described him at 24:

His Majesty is the handsomest potentate I ever set eyes on; above the usual height, with an extremely fine calf to his leg, his complexion very fair and bright, with auburn hair combed straight and short, in the French fashion, his throat being rather long and thick. He speaks French, English, and Latin, and a little Italian, plays well on the lute and harpsichord, sings from books at sight, draws the bow with greater strength than any man in England, and jousts marvelously. Believe me, he is in every respect a most accomplished Prince.

So as well as everything else, Henry could sing and play instruments. It is said that he owned 10 trombones, 14 trumpets, five bagpipes, 76 recorders and 78 flutes. And he certainly composed a range of songs that were sung at court, including the excellent 'Pastyme With Goode Company'.

Nevertheless, any association between King Henry and 'Greensleeves' has to remain in the realm of speculation. It is possible that King Henry knew the tune, and might even have created words to fit it, but nobody actually knows. There is not a single mention of 'Greensleeves' in the voluminous paperwork arising out of the king's 38-year reign. And Henry's life was well over long before any evidence of the song's existence came to light.

Definite knowledge about the song starts from 1580 – King Henry had died in 1547 – when Richard Jones, a printer, was issued with a licence to print 'A new Northern Dittye of the Lady Greene Sleeves'. On that same day, another printer named Edward White also had a licence issued for 'A ballad, being the Ladie Greene Sleeves'. It took four years to sort out the tussle about who had the printing rights; this was apparently settled in favour of Jones, since his was the first known printing of the song in 1584. It appeared in a collection called *A Handful of Pleasant Delights*, with the song described as 'A Courtly Sonnet to the Lady Greensleeves'. At the time the description 'sonnet' did not necessarily mean the formal 14-line structure that developed later. A sonnet could be any short lyrical piece of verse: this 'original' 'Greensleeves' had 18 10-line verses, which may have seemed short in that less frantic century. The lyrics were virtually the same as we know them now.

A British fiddle solo published in 1744 and called 'Piss on the Grass' was brought to prominence by a young dancer called Nancy Dawson, who made an explosive debut on the London stage in 1759 dancing to the tune. The tune was politely re-named as 'Nancy Dawson's Hornpipe'. In time, two different sets of words were grafted onto the old dance tune: 'I Saw Three Ships' and 'Here We Go Round the Mulberry Bush'.

The latter words are believed to have originated as a British working song sung by Yorkshire prisoners during the early days of Wakefield Prison, which began as a correction house in 1595, when they exercised by marching around a courtyard mulberry tree – which is still there. The old melody was aired in an unexpected context when Edward Albee's play *Who's Afraid of Virginia Woolf?* was made into a film. On stage, the play had used the tune 'Who's Afraid of the Big Bad Wolf?' from a Disney animated film called *The Three Little Pigs*. But reusing the tune in a movie required a larger royalty payment, so the old 'Mulberry' tune, which happened to fit the *Virginia Woolf* lyrics, was used instead.

The song quickly went into circulation, and was a palpable hit. Minus words, the popular melody was published in arrangements for lute, virginals and other instruments of the era. By 1599 the song was so well known that it is referred to in Shakespeare's *Merry Wives of Windsor*. Upon seeing his two prospective dates, Falstaff bellows, 'Let the sky rain potatoes; let it thunder to the tune of "Green Sleeves".' (He wasn't hungry: Elizabethans had an idea that potatoes were an aphrodisiac.)

Over time, countless varieties of words were sung to the same tune, especially during times of political upheaval in Britain. During the Civil War in the 17th century, the Cavaliers hijacked the tune in order to put about at least 14 different parodies with references relevant to the times. 'Greensleeves' then turned up in John Gay's famous *Beggars Opera* of 1728, which also featured a lot of other 'borrowed' tunes.

The 'Greensleeves' melody was sometimes attached to words with a Christian theme, such as the Christmas/New Year carol 'The Old Year Now Away Has Fled' of 1642. One such pious version which has enjoyed great success arose from a poem called 'The Manger Throne', written in 1865 by English poet William Chatterton Dix. Someone unknown took three verses of Dix's poem, and fitted them to the tune of 'Greensleeves'. The result was an immediately popular carol called 'What Child is This?'.

Despite its appearance in so many guises, there was a period when 'Greensleeves' was taken for granted and no longer the hit that it once had been. But Ralph Vaughan Williams' 1931 opera *Sir John in Love* (based on *The Merry Wives of Windsor*) used the old tune in charming ways, and an orchestral adaptation known as 'Fantasia on Greensleeves' proved a popular concert item. 'Greensleeves' was back in the public consciousness. Since then there have been multiple adaptations, sometimes using the original words, sometimes not. Leonard Cohen recorded a somewhat 'frank' variation, and the Smothers Brothers came out with 'Where the Lilac Grows', set to the old tune. The tune featured throughout the movie *How the West was Won*, with Debbie Reynolds singing yet another new version of the lyrics. There have also been jazz versions and reggae.

Michael Flanders and Donald Swann, whose 1956 theatre piece *At the Drop of a Hat* was enormously popular and ran for years, sang ' *Greensleeves'*, with a fanciful explanation that it had been composed by Henry VIII, and always raised a laugh on their final line: 'and the royalties go to royalty!'.

In spite of the many variations throughout the centuries, in contemporary times the preferred lyrics are those published in 1584. 'Greensleeves' has sometimes been called the world's favourite love song, which is hard to prove, but there's no question about its versatility: there can't be many ancient melodies that have been rearranged by both Ralph Vaughan Williams and John Coltrane.

> Alas, my love you do me wrong
> To cast me off discourteously
> And I have loved you so long
> Delighting in your company.
> *Chorus:*
> Greensleeves was all my joy
> Greensleeves was my delight
> Greensleeves was my heart of gold
> And who but my Lady Greensleeves.
>
> I have been ready at your hand
> to grant whatever you would crave;
> I have both wagered life and land
> Your love and good will for to have.
> *Chorus*
>
> I bought the kerchers* to thy head
> That were wrought fine and gallantly,
> I kept thee both at board and bed
> Which cost my purse well favouredly.
> *Chorus*
>
> Greensleeves now farewell! adieu!
> God I pray to prosper thee;
> For I am still thy lover true
> Come once again and love me.
> *Chorus*

* *kercher* – archaic version of kerchief, meaning a cloth or scarf placed over or around the head or neck (from the French couvre-chef, to cover the head).

What Child is This?

(to the tune 'Greensleeves')

What child is this who laid to rest
On Mary's lap is sleeping?
Whom angels greet with anthems sweet
While shepherds watch are keeping.
This, this is Christ the King
Whom shepherds guard and angels sing
Haste, haste to bring him laud
The babe, the son of Mary.

Why lies he in such mean estate
Where ox and ass are feeding?
Good Christian fear, for sinners here
The silent word is pleading
Nails, spear shall pierce him through
The cross be borne for me, for you
Hail, hail the Word made flesh
The babe, the son of Mary.

Then bring him incense, gold and myrrh
Come peasant, king to own him
The King of kings salvation brings
Let loving hearts enthrone him
Raise, raise the song on high
The virgin sings her lullaby
Joy, joy, for Christ is born
The babe, the son of Mary.

The Loveliest Night of the Year

When you are in love,
It's the loveliest night of the year.

JUVENTINO DE ROSAS, IRVING AARONSON, PAUL FRANCIS WEBSTER, 1950

Mario Lanza might never have heard of the Otimi people, but one of them provided him with a hit. Among these 'Indians' living in 19th-century Mexico was Juventino de Rosas, born in 1868. His father ran an itinerant street band and the boy grew up in Mexico City wandering with the group, learning to play the violin. He graduated to an opera house orchestra and eventually set out as a freelance musician, conductor and composer.

At only 19, Juventino de Rosas got himself to the World's Fair in New Orleans, where he first played a tune he'd composed, a lilting waltz reminiscent of skimming across rippling water. Hence its name, 'Sobre las Olas' (Over the Waves). The piece was published in 1891 and rapidly became popular among street performers, especially fiddlers in Mexico and Italian accordion players in New York. Juventino de Rosas was acknowledged as 'The Mexican Waltz King'. When his melody reached Europe, it was published as a piano solo under the German title 'Überwellen' (Over the Waves), giving rise to a popular misconception that the music was Viennese, from the Strauss waltz school.

Over 50 years after the melody was published, an extraordinary voice was gaining attention in Hollywood. This was the tenor Mario Lanza, whose first two movies catapulted him to international stardom. Decades later, star tenors Luciano Pavarotti, Placido Domingo and José Carreras, all acknowledged that hearing Lanza's singing when they were young had inspired them to pursue operatic careers. Lanza's particular hero was Enrico Caruso, and the American tenor's rapid success on screen resulted in preparations for him to star in a movie version of Caruso's life, to be called *The Great Caruso*. Thirty-year-old Lanza would of course sing appropriate operatic excerpts, but the movie-makers felt the need to include a gentle love ballad – and the movie's co-star, Ann Blyth, was herself a capable soprano. Juventino de Rosas's melody 'Over the Waves' came to the attention of the movie's music director, and its flowing legato and the length of its phrases indicated that if it had words, the melody would be eminently singable. Words were invented by Paul Francis Webster and 'Over the Waves' became 'The Loveliest Night of the Year'.

Soprano Ann Blyth debuted 'The Loveliest Night of the Year' in the film The Great Caruso, *1951.*

Memory has played tricks about the song's movie debut, however, for it was not, as many people believe, sung by Lanza, but by Ann Blyth as Dorothy Caruso, singing *to* Lanza. During 1950 Blyth recorded her performance for the film soundtrack. A few months later, early in 1951, before the movie was released, Lanza, recognising how effective the tune was, made a separate recording of his own version. This was released at the same time as the movie, and went straight onto the bestseller charts, where it remained for 34 weeks.

For whatever reason, though Ann Blyth sang 'The Loveliest Night of the Year' in the movie, her performance of the song did not appear on *The Great Caruso* album, and the song became indelibly associated with Lanza. Alas, Blyth's endearing performance was all but forgotten, though for many years her portrait shared the sheet music cover with Lanza's. In 1958 Lanza sang 'The Loveliest Night of the Year' on screen for the first time in the movie, *The Seven Hills of Rome*.

Hail, hail, the gang's all here
What the deuce do we care.
Gilbert and Sullivan's famous operetta, *The Pirates of Penzance*, written in 1879, introduced the powerful chorus melody, 'Come, friends who plough the sea'.

Some 30 years later, the tune was hijacked to become the American camping song, 'Hail, hail, the gang's all here'.

Years later, an album of 'Latin American Classics' caused some surprise with its lush orchestral version of 'Sobre Las Olas', proudly claimed by Mexico. But sadly, Mexican native Juventino de Rosas, who created the melody, never had an inkling of how famous his tune would eventually become. He died of scarlet fever in 1894, at the age of 26.

Bali Ha'i

May call you, any night, any day.

RICHARD RODGERS, OSCAR HAMMERSTEIN II, 1949

James Michener's famous *Tales of the South Pacific*, published in 1947, won the following year's Pulitzer Prize for Literature. The book was inspired by Michener's war experiences as a lieutenant commander in the US Navy, particularly on the islands of Melanesia, especially Guadalcanal in the Solomons. And Michener told it as it was: it could hardly have been less glamorous.

But when Michener's book became a musical and then a movie, the term 'South Pacific' went into common terminology. Before this, if an image of exotic glamour was required, this was traditionally conjured by using the words 'South Seas Isles', which instantly evoked swaying palms and lovely brown maidens. 'South Pacific' was simply a geographic description. But the combination of Michener, composer Richard Rodgers, lyricist Oscar Hammerstein II and singer Mary Martin made the words 'South Pacific' into a passport to fantasy, at least for people in the Northern Hemisphere. Americans now use the phrase to describe an exotic semi-tropical world, even advertising Hawaii, actually in the North Pacific, as a destination for a 'glamorous sun-filled South Pacific vacation'. 'North Pacific' sounds like a railway; Hawaii *wants* to be in the South Pacific.

And the island of Bali Ha'i? It may not have existed at all, but according to the original story, Michener wanted us to think it was near Guadalcanal. According to one New Zealand serviceman who was in the area at the time, Michener once heard someone speak the name Ba'elele'a, a remote constituency of the Western Solomons, not known for its lifestyle attractions. The American liked the name and wrote it down on a cigarette packet, murmuring, 'That might come in useful some day.'

It certainly did, when he used the name, as Bali Ha'i, as the mystical island to which French wives and children were sent for safety during the Second World War. But the retelling, first in the Rodgers and Hammerstein musical of 1949 and then in the 1958 movie, considerably blurred Michener's original images.

When Richard Rodgers first read *Tales of the South Pacific* he was concerned that the story of Bloody Mary, her Oriental daughter and an American naval man, was a bit too similar to *Madama Butterfly*, so the emphasis was shifted to two other characters: the nurse Nellie Forbush and her French admirer. Then producers of the stage show made a subtle scenic shift eastwards. Michener's original Melanesian settings, and the locals who lived there, were deemed insufficiently attractive, so the stage production featured softer-hued Polynesians. Michener may not have agreed. He wrote that young Melanesian women 'looked like models awaiting the immortalising brush of Gauguin. Unaware of their forbidding ugliness by American middle class standards, they were equally unaware of their surpassing beauty by the artist's immortal standards.'

And radical changes were wrought in Bloody Mary. Far from being amusing, jolly, large, and black, Michener's original Bloody Mary, who is believed to have been a real person, was very small, old, ugly and outlandish. She was a tough-minded marketeer with horrific language and a vile addiction to betel nut, which she chewed until the juice ran in red rivers from the corners of her mouth to the chin – hence the bloody part of her name; all foreign matrons were called 'Mary' by the American servicemen. Her original home was a village 'eighty miles from Hanoi', for Bloody Mary was not a buxom Polynesian or Afro-American, she was an Oriental, a Tonkinese – for which, after the reunification of 1946, read Vietnamese.

Nevertheless, within the musical's story, the Bloody Mary character was to be given the responsibility of establishing that Bali Ha'i was a mystical and revered place. Both Rodgers and Hammerstein felt that a song was needed to pin down the image of the island for the audience. Stanley Green's *Encyclopaedia of the Musical* tells that Hammerstein completed the lyrics to the song 'Bali Ha'i' and took them to Rodgers, who was in the middle of lunch. The composer pushed the dinner dishes to one side, read the words, turned the paper over and without hesitation composed the song straight onto the reverse side of the lyrics. Then he finished his meal. That song became a classic.

South Pacific opened in New York in April, 1949 starring Mary Martin as Nurse Nellie Forbush. At the conclusion of the premiere, the audience crowded into the aisles and cheered. Journalist Walter Winchell described it as 'South Terrific'. During its run the show earned nine Tonys and the Pulitzer Prize for Drama. As Bloody Mary, the Afro-American singer-actress Juanita Hall was an audience favourite, and her song, 'Bali Ha'i', quickly moved towards icon status. Nine years later, Hall was engaged to recreate her role on screen but her songs were dubbed with the glorious voice of Muriel Smith, who was the original Carmen Jones and had been London's Bloody Mary. She had also, curiously, screen-dubbed the singing voice of Zsa Zsa Gabor.

Almost immediately after the movie was released, the mystery became a hot topic: where was the real Bali Ha'i? The stage show had already spawned business enterprises named Bali Ha'i in the Pacific area but after the film came out serious boasting began about where the 'original' Bali Ha'i was located, or at least where it was filmed. In fact, the boar's tooth dance ceremony, and all the other action on Bali Ha'i, was filmed in studios on Santa Monica Boulevard in Hollywood, by performers who never set foot outside California.

Many islands wished they were Bali Ha'i, especially for the purpose of attracting tourists. Kauai, Moorea and Bora Bora tour guides will all tell you that their home is Bali Ha'i. True, Kauai and Moorea were film locations for part of the movie, and Bora Bora boasted a restaurant named Bloody Mary, but Kauai is a Hawaiian island in the North Pacific, and both Moorea and Bora Bora are in the Tahitian archipelago of French Polynesia, whereas the native population of Bali Ha'i was Melanesian and Tonkinese-Vietnamese.

The famous Hawaiian song 'Aloha E' was written by the country's queen, Her Majesty Queen Liliuokalani (1838–1917). A talented musician, she composed several successful songs.

One basis for Tahiti's claim to 'own' Bali Ha'i seems to be the few seconds of film showing an exterior view of a mountainous tree-rich island, claimed by Tahitians to show part of their territory. But another claim is that those significant few seconds of film are actually a view of Tioman, a thickly forested island off the coast of peninsular Malaysia.

Whatever the truth, the magic words Bali Ha'i still served to name various holiday cruises, hotels, restaurants, golf courses, scuba diving programmes and cocktails both south and north of the equator.

James Michener tried to set the record straight in an article he wrote for the *Philadelphia Sunday Bulletin* in 1970. He revealed that his image of Bali Ha'i was much closer to New Guinea than to Tahiti. In his creative mind, it was the combination of a 'miserable' village on Mono Island, about 400 miles north-west of Guadalcanal in the Solomon Islands, and a 'steaming, savage island called Aoba [now known as Ambae], in what is now Vanuatu. Michener confessed that those islands were so off-putting that no sane person would willingly visit them. As a writer, he had taken 'the privilege of dressing them up a little ... creating an island of loveliness and imagination named Bali Ha'i' – thus making it clear that no real Bali Ha'i ever existed. Perhaps the lure of Bali Ha'i is that it can be pictured any way you want. That's the power of fiction. 'I no longer know what the relationship between fact and fiction is, or ought to be,' Michener wrote. 'All I know is that I created an idea long before I saw its reality, and I believe that often happens in art.' And Hammerstein's words exactly capture the need for us all to dream in our imagination, of a 'special island'.

The original semi-autobiographical *Tales of the South Pacific* was based on truth, but the musical version prettied up the stories, without a hint of typhoons, noxious beetles or enemy shrapnel. After all, a stage musical featuring the genuine horrors of war, including dysentery and cockroaches, could hardly be regarded as a nice night out. In the 1960s, when Vietnam became a highly sensitive word, references to Bloody Mary being 'Tonkinese' were discreetly dropped from some productions. But her song continued to enchant. Bali Ha'i, Michener's island of loveliness and imagination, had become the new Shangri La.

You Don't Have To Say You Love Me

Just be close at hand.

Pino Donaggio, Vito Pallavicini, Simon Napier-Bell, Vicki Wickham, 1966

Mary O'Brien was a rather bland name. The plangent singing voice of a London teenager so named might never have made an impact on the world had she not learned to live without spectacles and become Dusty Springfield.

After a start as a vocalist in a group called the Lana Sisters, Dusty joined her brother, Dion O'Brien, who, under the name Tom Springfield, had an established band. Dusty gradually became the solo spot, then a solo star and eventually became known to the music press as 'the first of the pop divas'.'

In 1965 Dusty Springfield was invited to sing in the San Remo Festival, then the world's biggest song showcase and a wonderful platform for singers and for new songs. One night, Springfield went to hear the Italian singer/songwriter, Pino Donaggio. When he sang his own song 'Io Che non Vivo Senza Te' (I Can't Live Without You), the young British singer was powerfully affected by the melody, even though she didn't understand a word of the lyrics. Sitting as the audience stood and applauded, she dissolved into tears.

That Donaggio had produced such a strong piece was no surprise to an Italian audience. A well-known songwriter-singer, he had been trained rigidly as a classical musician, making his public debut at 14 as solo violinist playing Vivaldi. He went on to join the Solisti di Milano and was a respected classical violinist, until he met Canadian singer and composer Paul Anka, who represented a kind of music with which Donaggio had previously had no contact. A new world opened up, and the Italian abandoned classical for 'classical pop'. His standing in Italy was excellent, but it was Dusty Springfield who made one of his creations international – and brought him royalties for years to come.

Donaggio's song went back to England with Springfield, in the form of an acetate record disc. She was in no hurry, but was aware that as the 1960s grew older, record buyers might be ready for a big ballad, and it wouldn't do her career any harm if she were to provide it.

A year after returning from San Remo, Springfield spoke to her friend Vicki Wickham, who was producer of the influential British television show, *Ready Steady Go!*, a key element in the British pop music industry. She explained that she had been mulling over an Italian tune for a while and felt the need to record it but needed English lyrics. Wickham contacted Simon Napier-Bell, who then ran a small company making TV commercials and documentaries, but had expressed interest in getting into the music industry. Wickham suggested that providing lyrics for a star of Dusty Springfield's status would be a very good way to start.

The Italian tune became a definite part of Springfield's next recording session, and a new orchestral arrangement was organised. The lavish backing, with strings, brass, a choir, woodwind and percussion, had already been recorded. The next step would be to add the solo voice: the need for lyrics was urgent.

Napier-Bell later described the genesis of the English lyrics, making no secret of the role that his hedonistic lifestyle had played in their creation. He and Vicki Wickham met for a late dinner,

Dusty Springfield.

and then spent a desultory half-hour or so knocking suggested lyrics back and forth. Both agreed that the Italian flavour of the melody suggested a romantic feel but they argued about whether to begin with 'I love you', 'I don't love you' or even 'You don't love me'. That rather stark statement was softened to 'You don't have to love me' but they realised the words didn't fit the existing tune. So the statement was modified to 'You don't have to *say* you love me', which fitted the opening melody line very well.

Comforted by having written one line, and broken the first barrier, the pair stepped into a taxi and headed for a nightclub. By the time they arrived, the rest of the words had been composed. But because the evening's work had delayed his usual nocturnal clubbing, Napier-Bell decided that lyric-writing no longer appealed to him: it messed up his customary carousing.

The new words were delivered to Dusty Springfield scribbled onto the back of an envelope. Given the manner in which they had been thought up, it is no surprise that Dusty and her producer were at first dubious. But Wickham and Napier-Bell, who had both come to the recording session, were amazed that the combination of their perfunctory words, the tune and Dusty's voice melded so perfectly.

The singer herself was dissatisfied: to her, the playbacks sounded dead, because of the sound quality the low-ceilinged studio was delivering to tape. Her sound engineer, running from one floor to another, noticed that there was a pleasing ambience in the building's stairwell and suggested they try one take from there. He hung a microphone from the roof and Dusty stood on the steps and sang. The result was perfect.

The track, released in 1966, was a multi-million-selling chart-topper for Dusty Springfield. The unique combination of the plaintiveness, strength and passion of her voice worked brilliantly with the vibrant Italian tune and the simple English lyrics, which could well have sounded banal sung by anyone else.

'You Don't Have to Say You Love Me' remained virtually her theme song until her untimely death in 1999. The original composer, Donaggio, and the lyric writers benefited from its continual sales, which were boosted when Elvis Presley released his cover version in 1971. In later years, Dusty underplayed her own initial faith about her Italian discovery and referred to the song as 'good old schmaltz'. Schmaltz or not, it sold 60 million copies.

It's a Long Way to Tipperary

It's a long way to Tipperary,
It's a long way to go.

JACK JUDGE, HARRY WILLIAMS, 1912

Jack Judge had two ways of earning a living. By day he ran a stall in a fish market, and by night he sang in the music halls. He had a boyhood friend called Harry Williams, who now kept a country tavern called The Malt Shovel in Oldbury, near Birmingham, from where they both came. Judge sometimes found the going hard, financially, and Williams was always ready to help by making a loan available. Jack Judge had something of a knack for composing, and he promised his friend that if ever he wrote a best-selling song, he would put Harry Williams' name on it.

One of Judge's early efforts at a song was called 'How Are Ye?' and one night in 1912, when he was singing at the Grand Theatre in Stalybridge, he went to a nearby pub after the performance. There the locals ribbed him good naturedly about 'How Are Ye?' and his being a songwriter. A bet arose that he could not write a song the next day, and sing it on stage that same night. The stake was 5 shillings, which then would have bought a whole bottle of whisky and several dozen cigarettes. Jack Judge accepted the challenge, and late that night as he was leaving the pub, he overheard one man giving another directions, which began 'It's a long way to …'. The phrase stuck in his mind as he went to bed. And the next morning when he remembered the phrase, although he had never been to Ireland, out of the blue the word 'Tipperary' fell into place, and a classic was on the way.

That day Judge went to another local pub, the New Market Inn, and sat there composing the rest of the words, and the tune. He sang it to his friend Horace Vernon, who was musical director at the Grand Theatre, and Vernon went without lunch to make sure he had the notation of melody and accompaniment written down correctly. That night, 31 January 1912, Jack Judge won his bet, singing 'It's a Long Way to Tipperary' on stage at the Grand. A local businessman immediately offered to buy the copyright but, with sensible caution, Judge sensed a more widespread success. Feldman & Company in London took over the publishing of the song, with copyright royalties payable to Jack Judge – but not just him. He kept his promise to his friend by adding 'music by Harry Williams' to the copyright.

The song's first step towards national, and later international, fame happened when Florrie Forde sang it in a pantomime in 1914. Forde was a No.1 British star, queen of the music hall, and she had made major hits out of 'Down at the Old Bull and Bush' and 'Hold Your Hand Out You Naughty Boy'. To have her sing your song was a composer's dream. But another incident proved even more important, because of an observant journalist.

A hit of the same era, 'Keep the Home Fires Burning', was composed in 1914 by Ivor Novello (with words by Lena Ford) at the request of his mother, who found 'Tipperary' boring.

Within the British Army there was one battalion whose members were mostly from Ireland – the 7th Battalion, Connaught Rangers Regiment. These soldiers very quickly identified with the jaunty song about Tipperary. Many of them had been stationed there and knew the town well; some had sweethearts there. At evenings in the barracks, the mess often resounded with the strains of 'It's a Long Way to Tipperary', and new recruits were taught this Irish-sounding song – albeit composed by an Englishman from Birmingham.

After the declaration of war, the Connaught Rangers were among the British troops who sailed to France in August 1914. After a period in temporary barracks in the docklands of Boulogne, the soldiers marched through the town to new quarters in the hills. As they marched, each regiment sang its favourite song, such as 'Soldiers of the King', or 'Goodbye Dolly Gray' – and the Connaught Rangers sang 'It's a Long Way to Tipperary'.

George Turnock, a journalist representing England's *Daily Mail*, was standing in the street. Most of the other songs were familiar, but he had never heard 'Tipperary' before. A French war widow standing next to him asked what the words meant. When he got as far as 'it's a long way to go', she was overcome, and replied in French, 'Those poor young men. War is indeed a long way to go.' Turnock's despatch about the British troops arriving in France mentioned only one song, 'Tipperary'.

From some places, it's not such a long way to Tipperary.

From then, the song's fame grew. Reprintings of the sheet music (there were many) bore the sub-heading 'The Marching Anthem on the Battlefields of Europe, Sung by The Soldiers Of The King'. And the statement was close to the truth. Different regiments had other songs they treasured, but 'Tipperary' overcame all barriers and was sung and enjoyed by military and civilians alike throughout the war. Chinese war workers in France sang it; eventually Germans sang it too. When peace arrived, the song went home with troops from Canada, Australia, India and New Zealand.

In Ireland, the town of Tipperary welcomed the attention and pragmatically accepted that their name had been made world famous by a man who'd never been there. The Grand Theatre in Stalybridge where Judge first sang the song was later renamed the Hippodrome, and then later a café named the Tipperary Tea Room was opened there.

The song's fame and its sales were encouraged by war, but there were many throughout those grim years, and afterwards, whose spirits were lifted by the cheerful optimism of 'It's a Long Way to Tipperary'. Harry Williams' generosity and Jack Judge's loyalty were both rewarded: both men accrued very significant royalties, and lived in more comfort than they ever had before.

The original 1912 words (bearing in mind that gay meant happy and lively then):

Up to mighty London came an Irishman one day,
As the streets are paved with gold, sure ev'ryone was gay;
Singing songs of Piccadilly, Strand and Leicester Square,
'Til Paddy got excited, then he shouted to them there:
Chorus:
It's a long way to Tipperary, it's a long way to go;
It's a long way to Tipperary, to the sweetest girl I know;
Good-bye Piccadilly, farewell Leicester Square,
It's a long, long way to Tipperary, but my heart's right there.

Paddy wrote a letter to his Irish Molly O',
Saying, 'Should you not receive it, write and let me know!
If I make mistakes in spelling, Molly, dear,' said he,
'Remember it's the pen that's bad, don't lay the blame on me.'
Chorus

Molly wrote a neat reply to Irish Paddy O',
Saying, 'Mike Maloney wants to marry me, and so
Leave the Strand and Piccadilly, or you'll be to blame,
For love has fairly drove me silly, hoping you're the same.'
Chorus

Bibliography

Banfield, Stephen. *Sondheim's Broadway Musicals*, University of Michigan Press, 1993.

The Blue Angel, introduction by Josef von Sternberg, Classic Film Scripts, Simon & Schuster, New York, 1968,

Cantrick, Robert B. 'The Blind Man and the Elephant', *Ethnomusicology Journal*, Vol. 9, No. 2, 1965.

Cats – the book of the musical, Faber & Faber, 1981.

Gerald Clarke, *Get Happy: The life of Judy Garland*, Warner Books, 2000.

Coveney, Michael. *Cats on a Chandelier*, Hutchinson, London, 1999.

Coward, Noel. *Present Indicative*, Methuen, London, 1986.

Anne Edwards, *Judy Garland, a Biography*, Simon & Schuster, New York, 1975.

Clive Fisher. *Noel Coward*, Weidenfeld & Nicolson, London, 1992.

Fuld, James. *The Book of World Famous Music*, Dover Publications, New York, 1985.

Gammond, Peter (ed.). *The Oxford Companion to Popular Music*, Oxford University Press, New York, 1993.

Jean Garceau with Inez Cocke. *Dear Mr. G – the biography of Clark Gable*, Little Brown & Co., Boston, 1961.

Harrison, Rex, *Rex*, Macmillan London, 1974.

Harrowven, Jean. *Origins of Rhymes, Songs and Sayings*, Kaye & Ward, London, 1979.

Jean Howard, *Travels with Cole Porter*, Harry Abrams, New York, 1991.

Kimball, Robert (ed.) and Brendan Gill. *Cole*, Michael Joseph, London, 1987.

Lerner, Alan Jay. *The Street Where I Live*, Hodder & Stoughton, London, 1978.

Lisle, Tim de (ed.). *Lives of the Great Songs*, Pavilion, London, 1994.

Nettel, Reginald. *Seven Centuries of Popular Song*, Phoenix House Ltd, London, 1956.

Riva, Maria. *Marlene Dietrich*, Alfred A. Knopf, New York, 1992.

Scholes, Percy (ed.). *The Oxford Companion to Music*, Oxford University Press, London, 1960.

Shipman, David. *Judy Garland*, HarperCollins, Canada, 1992.

Steyn, Mark. *Broadway Babies Say Goodnight*, Faber & Faber, London, 1997.

Joseph P. Swain. *The Broadway Musical: A Critical and Musical Survey*, Oxford University Press, London and New York, 1990.

Wilk, Max. *They're Playing Our Song*, W.H. Allen, London, 1974.

Zadan, Craig. *Sondheim & Co.*, Pavilion Books, 1987.

Acknowledgements

As provided by Australasian Mechanical Copyright Owners Society, the copyright for songs quoted is held by:

'Memory', T. S. Eliot, Trevor Nunn, Andrew Lloyd Webber, Universal
'Love Me Tender', George R. Poulton, Vera Matson, Elvis Presley, EMI 80% /Universal 20%
'Edelweiss', Richard Rodgers, Oscar Hammerstein II, EMI
'Hello Dolly', Jerry Herman, Warner Chappell
'Lili Marlene', Norbert Schultze, GEMA affiliated society in Germany
'Somewhere Over the Rainbow', Harold Arlen, E.Y. Harburg, J. Albert & Sons Pty Ltd
'Yesterday', Paul McCartney, EMI/Sony
'White Christmas', Irving Berlin, EMI
'Moon River', Johnny Mercer, Henry Mancini, BMG
'Begin the Beguine', Cole Porter, Warner Chappell
'I Don't Know How to Love Him', Tim Rice, Andrew Lloyd Webber, Universal
'Rudolph the Red-nosed Reindeer, Robert May, Johnny Marks, Warner Chappell
'I Could Have Danced All Night', Alan Jay Lerner, Frederick Loewe, Warner Chappell
'Blue Moon', Richard Rodger, Lorenz Hart, J. Albert & Sons Pty Ltd
'Beyond the Blue Horizon', Leo Robin, Richard A. Whiting, W. Franke Harling, BMG
'Mad Dogs and Englishmen', Noel Coward, Chappell and Co.
'Falling in Love Again', Friedrich Hollaender, Sammy Lerner, Hello Mr Wilson/BUG
'Candle in the Wind', Elton John, Bernie Taupin, Universal
'Send in the Clowns', Stephen Sondheim, Hugh Wheeler, Warner Chappell
'The Loveliest Night of the Year', Juventino de Rosas, Irving Aaronson, Paul Francis Webster, Universal/EMI
'You Don't Have to Say You Love Me', Pino Donaggio, Vito Pallavicini, Simon Napier-Bell, Vicki Wickham, EMI
'Bali Ha'i', Richard Rodgers, Oscar Hammerstein II, EMI